W9-CCY-507

THE
WEALTHY
BODY IN
BUSINESS

THE WEALTHY BODY IN BUSINESS

EARN MORE MONEY BY BEING IN BETTER SHAPE

Tim Bean and Anne Laing

Green
Tree

BLOOMSBURY

LONDON · OXFORD · NEW YORK · NEW DELHI · SYDNEY

Green Tree
An imprint of Bloomsbury Publishing Plc

50 Bedford Square
London
WC1B 3DP
UK

1385 Broadway
New York
NY 10018
USA

www.bloomsbury.com

BLOOMSBURY and the Diana logo are trademarks of Bloomsbury Publishing Plc

First published in 2017

© Tim Bean and Anne Laing, 2017

Illustrations © Dave Saunders

Tim Bean and Anne Laing have asserted their right under the Copyright, Designs and Patents Act, 1988, to be identified as the Authors of this work.

All rights reserved. No part of this publication may be reproduced or transmitted in any form or by any means, electronic or mechanical, including photocopying, recording, or any information storage or retrieval system, without prior permission in writing from the publishers.

Disclaimer: The information contained in this book is a) correct, to the best of the authors' and publisher's knowledge, at the date of publication; and b) published for general information purposes only and does not constitute medical or other professional advice on any subject matter. In no way are there any expressed or implied representations by the authors or publisher that the information contained in this book constitutes or is a substitute for medical advice or guidance by a qualified doctor. The authors and publisher employees do not accept any responsibility for any loss, which may arise from reliance on information contained in this book.

British Library Cataloguing-in-Publication Data

A catalogue record for this book is available from the British Library.

Library of Congress Cataloguing-in-Publication data has been applied for.

ISBN: Trade Paperback: 9781472935144
ePub: 9781472935151
ePDF: 9781472935168

2 4 6 8 10 9 7 5 3 1

Typeset in ITC Galliard by Deanta Global Publishing Services, Chennai, India
Printed and bound in Great Britain by CPI Group (UK) Ltd, Croydon, CR0 4YY

FSC
www.fsc.org
MIX
Paper from
responsible sources
FSC® C020471

To find out more about our authors and books visit www.bloomsbury.com.
Here you will find extracts, author interviews, details of forthcoming
events and the option to sign up for our newsletters.

To

George & William

Cardea & William

Harrison & Edward

Matthew

Carry on the wisdom to make the world a healthier place

TABLE OF CONTENTS

ENDORSEMENTS

'What can I say about *The Wealthy Body?* We often hear words like "body image" and "nutrition" thrown around, but these words will not be important to you if you are on the first steps of the road I am travelling (and in due course I hope you will soon be!), so I shall try to tell you briefly what this has done for me:

1. I need glasses that are only half as strong as they were last year.
2. I no longer wonder whether I can walk to the tube station but how fast I can run 5 miles.
3. People have respect for me as soon as I walk into a room, not just after I open my mouth and start talking.
4. People ask me my advice on health and fitness.
5. My friends tell me I look ten years younger.
6. I look for the stairs, not for a lift, and people cannot keep up with me if they walk beside me.
7. I no longer want to keep my shirt on at the beach, but rather have a Spartan '300' beach body (Next year, Tim!).
8. I can go to designer clothes shops (not just to the tailor) and buy clothes off-the-rack.
9. I got a job offer based on my 'energy and drive'. Before meeting Tim I would have endured the (unspoken) interview question, *Why are you so fat?*
10. When someone looks at me, I know what they are thinking … and it's not, *Boy, he's let himself go…*

It's the best investment I have ever made and has given me my life back at the age of 40. I intend to live the rest of it to the fullest.'

Jonathan Biles, CEO,
Gate Insurance Group

'Truly revolutionary on many levels. Having seen first-hand the problems of "burn-out" and general "wellness" issues, particularly at the most senior

xii | The Wealthy Body in Business

levels at the firm, I think this book offers a unique and sustainable answer to the issues our most important – and busiest – senior managers face.'

Dame Amelia Fawcett, DBE,
Former Vice Chairman & COO (Morgan Stanley International)

'As scientists and physicians, we know the ageing process in men and women is complex. In many different ways, the body gradually ceases to operate as optimally as it did when it was younger. Most often we can view this as an accumulation of physiological errors that did not exist in our earlier years. However, although no one can stop the process of getting chronologically older, there is much that can be done to halt or even reverse the damage caused by lifestyle factors.

For many years, Tim Bean and Anne Laing have been changing the lives and lifestyles of men and women who face the daily challenges of corporate life. They have combined their deep understanding of the business community with a physiological approach to proactive wellness. Their approach blends best practices in exercise, nutrition, regeneration and restorative medicine, and integrates these into the high-pressure corporate lifestyle.

This book presents the case for executive well-being in a practical and sensible manner, yet has been written from the heart using real stories about real people. It exposes common health issues and offers realistic solutions. It goes beyond the boundaries of traditional wellness programmes by offering a fully rounded approach and I applaud what the authors have set out to achieve.

I trust you will enjoy reading this book, and I hope you take full advantage of the wisdom and information it contains.'

Dr Sergey Dzugan
M.D. PhD

'Tim Bean has, singlehandedly, become the spark that has ignited my desire to have a healthy mind and body that supports my career and family aspirations. A picture of health himself, Tim's work is based on science and years of experience. In this book, Tim and Anne Laing share countless insights and actionable advice that can help anyone experience the benefits of good health. Executives in particular should pay careful attention to chapters about the brain-body connection, corporate career killers, and ageing. These authors know their material and I am pleased to see their insights now available to us all.'

Prof Dr Michael Netzley, Academic Director,
SMU-ExD Executive Development, Singapore

INTRODUCTION: WHY THIS BOOK?

The business world is getting tougher rather than easier, faster rather than slower, and more stressful rather than less. The city is uploading more pressure, and companies are downsizing their key talent.

Yet none of us are getting any younger. Instead of getting stronger, fitter, faster, more energised and engaged, we're mostly getting older, slower, weaker, softer, fatter and sicker as we age. At senior levels the gap between expectations to lead and perform, and the ability and capacity to do so, is ever widening.

Something has to give – and it is. People in business are crumbling under the load, fading under the pressure, and dying under their desks. It's true. You know it, and you've probably seen it.

The cost to business, to family and to society is massive – incalculable even.

What can be done to close this mile-wide chasm afflicting millions of people at work?

That's what this book is all about.

The Wealthy Body in Business is a behind the scenes insight – an insider's guide, if you will – to the most successful strategies, tips and best practices we've been using successfully over the years with our private clients at the top levels of business. Executives, directors, leaders and luminaries – high-profile, high-flying men and women, entrepreneurs operating at the hard edge of business, where the pressures are enormous, the stakes are highest, and the cost of failure inconceivable.

In applying these simple but robust remedies, we've seen people get leaner, stronger, smarter, sharper, more confident, more agile, energised and a whole lot less stressed than they've ever been.

They're making better decisions, becoming better leaders, and extending their influence and earning capacity exponentially.

They're happier, healthier and more successful. They love the way they feel about life and about business. Their families love it, the staff enjoy it, and their doctors are quietly pleased (well, you'd hardly expect them to jump up and down, now would you?).

If this works for them, it will certainly work for you.

This powerful book is packed full of quick wins and easy-to-implement action points, and even if you put only a tenth of its ideas in place, we guarantee you'll notice a difference, and others around you will notice a difference too. People who are in better shape, with more energy, sleeping better, being less stressed, thinking smarter, feeling healthier, working better, always being on top of their game, will always be more successful in business, and in life.

We call it having The Wealthy Body, and it's yours for the taking...

1.
TOUGH LOVE

Let's start with a bit of straight talking. Getting healthy and staying healthy takes work. You live in a body that was designed to work hard, yet you live in a world where strenuous work is discouraged. We have lifts, escalators and cars to replace the tedium of physical movement, and food is easy to find, and easy to eat. It is over-processed too; we call it pre-chewed un-food. Businesspeople work at jobs that require very little physical movement, and we bathe our entire bodies in chemicals at the expense of our immune systems from the food we eat, the air we breathe and the products we put on our skin. See page 132 for more on preservatives and parabens in the everyday products we use.

We humans have managed to achieve the ultimate goal of evolution: to find an easy way of staying alive with minimal exertion and a reduced chance of being killed by another life form, big or small. But Mother Nature has never been concerned with longevity. Her main objective is survival and the propagation of the species as a whole, not you specifically. We are programmed to survive into our twenties, at which point we're old enough to reproduce. Beyond that, we're on our own.

YOU represent the pinnacle of evolution. How about that?

So congratulate yourself. You represent the pinnacle of evolution. You! It makes you feel a little better when you look at yourself naked in the bathroom mirror, doesn't it?

No? Not really?

Well, that's because there's another side to this story. Although we as a species have attained a degree of evolutionary nirvana, our bodies didn't get the memo. They forgot to show up to the meeting, and as such we are all still walking around in last year's model. Well, actually, it's a little more than last year's model. The body, brain, nervous system, digestive system, reflexes, musculature and everything else that makes up 'you' and 'us' hasn't changed much in the last 100,000 years. The model you are wearing is used to scrabbling around looking for food that is really tough to chew and digest. It is used to walking many miles in search of this food, as well as for shelter and safety; and it is careful to store extra energy around the midsection for use in those lean months when food is nowhere to be seen. And it is used to movement. Lots of movement.

So when this old-model human body finds itself in the prosperous age of the twenty-first century, it has a hard time shifting gears. Our plentiful food supply is stored as efficiently as ever – as fat – wrapping itself securely around our waist, legs and organs. Meanwhile, our innate need to store energy makes it very easy to slide into a sedentary life where only the texting thumbs are kept busy.

So we – you – are up against a challenge.

Is There Any Good News in All of This?

Actually, it is all good news. Your body is a remarkable device. It has the power to heal and to take care of much of what comes its way. It listens and it learns. When you use it, it grows stronger and better. When you give it a chance to clean out the pollutants and replace them with healthy foods, it responds vigorously and rewards you with all kinds of perks, such as greater energy, vitality, sexual drive, charisma, better skin tone, vocal power and posture, clear thought, better memory, better sex, better sleep, longer life – the list goes on and on.

You can achieve all this, but it is hard, which makes perfect sense.

If it isn't hard, if it isn't tough, if it isn't a challenge, then greatness will not be achieved. To work your body means to move *against* the instinctive desire for rest, but to also move *with* the instinctive desire for health.

You were lucky enough, smart enough and quick enough to be born. You beat many millions of other sperm for that opportunity. You were clever enough and tough enough to survive the challenges and illnesses of childhood. And you are clever enough now to be interested in becoming a better person, or else you wouldn't be reading these words. Doesn't all this tell you something? Your body, mind and soul all want you to become the best person you can be, even if you don't consciously know it yet.

This book provides the insights you need to become aware of the fantastic power of being truly human, and to make it a permanent reality for you.

> **Wealthy Body Wisdom:** *A sharp mind and a lean body is an all-or-nothing proposition. You can't have one foot on the platform and one on the train – you know how that's going to play out...*

The Shape of Things to Come

What do you suppose it's going to take to get you back in shape? Into the kind of shape you've never been before in your life?

Think back across the history of your life. Was there a time when you were in good shape? Probably when you were young, with energy to spare. What were you doing at that time to maintain that sort of physical condition? Were you playing sport every day? Were you running, cycling, rowing? Were your growth and hormonal levels high?

They say that youth is wasted on the young, and that is so often true. So many young people take their health and vitality for granted. Many ignore it, some abuse it and others just believe it will last forever.

> *To change the result, you must change the data.*

Unfortunately though, people age. As you get older, and as you collect more and more sedentary years under your ever-expanding belt, you become less active, less strong, less able to commit the time it took to be fit. You become weaker, softer and fatter than your younger self.

It's a trap to think that a little change here and a little change there will be enough to reverse the damage that those years of sedentary living have wrought and bring you back into a fit and functional condition.

If you want to reshape your body, but are forced to remain in the sedentary environment you operate in today, something has to give. There has to be a point where you are prepared to commit total effort to adjusting the way you do things.

To change the result, you must change the data. If you want to be lean, you must cut out the things that make you soft and fat.

It's great if you want to cut down a little on bread, cheese, butter, wine and sugar, and to add a little exercise into the mix, and yes, this will produce some changes in your body. But you must understand that the degree of change you are prepared to make is always proportional to the degree of result you will get. Change a little – get a little. Change a lot – get a lot.

> **Wealthy Body Wisdom:** *The difference between hot water and steam is just 1 degree. Step up your game-plan – a little change makes a big difference!*

If you start walking and continue to walk, you will become fit enough to walk. But that's it. However, if you then push yourself on to a slow jog, and then to a run, there is no limit to how fit you will become because you will be constantly challenging yourself to improve. If you really want to get a result that will make a significant difference, then you must be prepared to sacrifice some of the things that have made you soft and fat, and embrace the things that will harden, toughen and define your physique and your mind in the way nature designed them to be.

You are not alone in wanting to make this happen. And you will not be alone in taking on the challenges and regimens required. And you want to know something else? You're not unique. Sure, you have schedules and conflicts, meetings and emails, a hellish commute, a family to deal with and way too much already demanding your time. But you know what? So does everyone else. It's all a matter of what you choose to do with your time; what you say yes to and what you say no to.

> *Being in great shape isn't about self-sacrifice – it's about self-respect.*

> *Wealthy Body Wisdom: What you eat and how you exercise today, will determine how you look and feel tomorrow...*

Read any biography of any successful CEO and you will see two items in common. First, they never fill their calendars to 100 per cent full. They know how to say *no* to tasks of lesser value, in order that they can focus on those items that yield the most; and secondly, they always factor time in for exercise.

This book teaches you how to get strong enough to achieve The Wealthy Body, just like thousands of the world's top CEOs who are already doing so. It's about both physical and mental toughness. It all boils down to what you want. Are you prepared to do it? Is it important enough to you to get it?

Really?

OK. Then here's a test for you . . .

Drop and do 20 push-ups right now.

Did you do it?

The only acceptable excuse at this point is if you are on a plane at this moment, in which case, you are permitted to do them in the Arrivals lounge later.

No other excuse is allowed.

Now you might be asking yourself, 'Why should I do 20 push-ups right now? Nobody can see me.'

Well, that's true. Only you know if you have done the push-ups. But if you want to get into shape, then you will have done those push-ups to satisfy no-one but yourself.

If you did those push-ups, your mind-set is already well on the way towards building The Wealthy Body.

If you did not do those push-ups, your mind is still in resistance mode, comfortable sitting atop those excess kilos of flesh, muscle and fat.

Not to worry. You can have another chance. Do them now.

Then we can move on to creating the body you've always wanted.

> *Wealthy Body Action Points: To help get you started...*
>
> *1. Join a gym. The most important criterion is making sure it's handy. The more convenient it is to get to, the better.*

2. Book a trainer. Ask to see client testimonials and before-and-after pictures, and ask to see their abs. Trainers simply knowing the theory isn't good enough – they should also believe it enough to follow it themselves. Make sure they have a system to log, track and improve every exercise in every workout to ensure your progress. Insist on having your measurements and fitness assessed regularly. You can't manage what you don't measure.

3. Clear out all the rubbish. Throw away all the food and drinks from your cupboards at home, and desk drawer at work, which you know you probably shouldn't be having. There are suggestions as to what to replace it with further on...

Wealthy Body Wisdom: *There are only two moments in life.* Now *and* Too late!

2.
THE WEALTHY BODY vs THE RAT RACE

The age of *Homo sapiens,* or Wise man, is an age in which the brain has taken over as the primary tool of survival. You can see that all other animals employ a balance of brain, senses and agility in order to stay alive and procreate. But we grew our brains large, and we gave ourselves a promotion, from hunter-gatherer to desk potato. Exercise has been engineered out of our lives at every turn, and ironically this now poses one of the biggest threats to our continued survival.

It's amazing that for all the intelligence we have identified in ourselves, we have made the fundamental mistake of considering two elements, brain and body, to be essentially separate. This is nonsense. The brain is part of the body just as the lungs, heart and liver are. This perceived anatomical disconnect not only damages our longevity but it also does bad things to our bank balance, especially when people fall for the messages in advertising – which are designed to bypass the brain entirely and appeal to more basic instincts of fear, shame and urgency, in order to sell.

The brain is just another organ of the body. The care you take in maintaining the rest of your body results in equal care being delivered to the brain.

> *You don't have to be ill to get better.*

Protecting and preserving what we call your cerebral capital is of utmost importance in avoiding one or more of the three corporate career killers: Burn-out, Bail-out or Booted out!

Consider the statement: *Anything you ever do from the neck up is dependent totally on everything you do from the neck down.* It's true. Your total capacity for performance will always be dependent on the lowest physiological denominator.

That is why we always prioritise essential body maintenance as a baseline, around which everything else must fit. In order to think better, in order to fit into that nice suit, in order to be the boardroom star, you need to build a body that is vibrant with abundant energy and vitality, free of disease and illnesses; a body optimised for a rich, long life where each day can be experienced with verve, energy and contentment.

This body, your own private model of The Wealthy Body, is not an unobtainable dream. It doesn't matter what your age. Too many people we speak to think it is too hard to change, but it isn't. It is a body that anyone can have at any age with the right knowledge, backed by good intent and a compelling reason.

Neuroscientists now have an exciting understanding of the biological relationship between the brain, the mind and the body. We see the results of effective training in the people we have worked with over the last 30 years. Their first comment, even before the inevitable weight loss and shape-change, is how they notice a definite feeling of being energised, clear-headed, focused and youthful.

> **Wealthy Body Wisdom:** Engage your brain before eating – each mouthful influences your psychology and physiology as it travels through the body. There is nothing you put in your mouth that has no consequence...

A Difficult Choice

Very recently I had an interesting conversation with one of our clients, a VP of a large investment bank. He had just made a major promotion decision.

He was selecting one of his executive team to head the division covering Europe, Middle East and Africa. The role would place the successful candidate under a lot of pressure, and this person would be required to travel extensively to cover the territory.

Our client was down to the final choice between two likely individuals, both extremely capable, and proven performers to boot.

On the one hand, Candidate A was obviously overweight. His diet consisted primarily of croissants, coffee, pasta and wine, and his exercise was almost non-existent. He smoked half a packet of cigarettes a day, and his breathing was audibly laboured. However, the man was a genius. As a manager he was a star performer, and as a strategic director he was gifted.

Candidate B also presented at a similar level – on paper. Again, an outstanding manager and top performer in every way, although slightly older than his rival. However, this candidate was clearly in great physical shape. He trained daily in the gym, played sports on the weekends, and was careful to eat a high-performance diet. He avoided soft drinks, alcohol and tobacco, and maintained a strict personal regime.

A choice had to be made, and my client asked me, 'So, which one do you think I picked?'

I could see the way this was heading, so volunteered, 'The fit guy?'

He smiled fleetingly and said, 'Yes, but not for the reasons you might think. You see it all came down to just one simple question. I sat down with Candidate A, and said, "Dave, if you have so clearly failed at looking after something as fundamentally important as your own health, how are you going to look after my global division?" And, crucially, he had no answer for that.

'At the end of the process, it wasn't about weight, it wasn't about diet, and it wasn't about exercise – because that's personal.'

He went on, 'In a role that requires longer hours, more pressure, more travel and greater stress, it doesn't matter how talented or experienced you are; if your health breaks down, you lose the capacity to function.

'You see it's all about risk: risk to the team, risk to the business and risk to the shareholders. But most importantly it's about risk to the individual and to his family. In a high-pressure position like this there's simply too much at stake, so I chose the candidate most likely to survive.'

Can You Afford to be Unhealthy?

Depending on where you are based, you may require medical insurance – and the cost of this continues to rise. Even if you do not have to pay such costs, do remember that illness has other impacts. What will it mean to you if you get sick? Downtime away from the office costs you in terms of career opportunity as well as income. Additional repercussions and side effects of prescription drugs can be deadly to your career, even if they actually keep you alive.

And what about the impact to the business? Team paralysis, loss of forward momentum, internal politics, drop in external brand value, loss of shareholder confidence, and damage to key client relationships. This is how sickness can cost your business millions.

It is a smart investment to take the time to learn the strategies that make your body operate at top performance levels.

> **Wealthy Body Wisdom:** Cheap foods go hand in hand with expensive health care.

> **Myth:** I don't have time to exercise or think about what I am going to eat.
>
> **A:** People who have more things going on in their lives find time to fit important things in. Their bodies are more energetic, their minds are thinking faster and they become very efficient at what they are doing.
>
> We all have the same 24 hours in a day – they aren't making any more – but this is not about time management.
>
> This is about managing your energy, and prioritising the things that will support that. Time spent on your health is not wasted, it's an essential investment in energy. Think of it like cleaning your teeth – it's a health and hygiene habit!

Better Health Means More Money in the Bank

So what exactly *is* The Wealthy Body? The Wealthy Body happens at two levels. At one level possessing great health is your most important asset in and of itself – one that becomes more valuable to you as you age. But at another level, being in great shape, with abundant vigour and energy, allows you to be more focused and driven, more charismatic and credible, and empowers you to operate in business at a higher level than your counterparts and adversaries. This affords you the capacity to generate much greater wealth for longer, in a fiscal, and social, sense.

> » It's about performing at your intellectual peak for longer.
> » It's about being able to stay in the game longer.

» It's also about keeping ahead of those young upstarts nipping at your heels.

We race through our days without thought for the vehicle that carries us there.

We survive on too little sleep, we start the day on coffee, we gulp food on the run and we unwind with alcohol. Most often this demand exceeds our physiological capacity and the various nuts and bolts start to loosen. We are stoked with calories yet we have no energy. Our to-do lists, smartphones and computers prompt us to work 24/7. The relentless demands of work make it difficult to stay focused and we end the day exhausted, irritable and tired, with little energy for family or time out.

> 'The doctor of the future will give no medicine, but will interest patients in the care of the human frame, in diet and in the cause and prevention of disease.' – Thomas A. Edison

Wealthy Body Wisdom: *Knowledge is power. You don't know what you don't know, and when you do find out what you didn't know before, it can be painful, but only then do you have the power to change.*

Presenteeism

Have you heard of presenteeism? It's when a person is physically at work but is mentally not there. Whether their mental absence is due to overload, fatigue, stress, poor sleep, poor health or a combination of these, you or your team members are mentally driving with the hand-brake still on.

Presenteeism costs. It affects your company, your career and your health. An unhealthy leader or team member creates instability and uncertainty within an organisation. Companies that spend their time and money to select and develop senior leaders have a right to expect their key people to be in the best possible health for that position.

Think about cars for a moment. You know that no matter what the make of car, you need to get the maintenance right. Otherwise, top speed and reliability vanish, and ending your journey prematurely is a strong possibility. All cars must have downtime for overhaul and specialised maintenance. It's the same for people.

I'm Comfortable with My Weight, Thank You

Are you the type to shrug your shoulders and accept your out-of-shape physique as an unavoidable reality of mid-life? Maybe you think having a big belly won't make you lose your mind. But you're wrong.

Men and women who have a big belly at the age of 50 are up to *300 per cent more likely* to suffer from dementia as they age, according to the American Academy of Neurology.[1]

There is another point to remember: looking good tells your clients that you take your health seriously enough to be of the best use to them and their organisations. By contrast, people who look unhealthy and run down tell a different story about the company they work for and the service they deliver. After all, if you cannot look after something as fundamental as your own physique, how can you look after the best interests of your organisation?

Wealthy Body Action Points

1. Take your waist circumference measurement 2.5cm (1 inch) above the navel. Men should measure less than 96cm (38 inches), and women less than 76cm (30 inches). Any measurement greater than these moves you into high-risk territory for many diseases, including heart attack, stroke, diabetes and dementia.

2. If you do not have a tape measure, lie down on your back and look down towards your feet. If your stomach sticks up higher than your chest, you need to lose weight ASAP.

3. If you are routinely blaming your dry-cleaner for shrinking the waistband of your trousers, it's time to face facts. It's not the trousers.

Myth: *I have about 35kg (80lb) to lose. Am I too far gone to see an improvement to my health?*

A: *Dozens of our clients have lost similar amounts. Every pound you lose is bringing you closer to a healthier physique. You're never, ever 'too far gone' to begin.*

The Problem of Congruence...

...and how one of the most important lessons in corporate performance doesn't come from the world of business, but from motor racing!

We recently worked alongside one of the teams in the British Touring Car Championships, having been brought in as consultants to optimise driver performance.

I remember my first visit to the headquarters, when their race director toured me through the facility. After a quick scan around the offices we emerged into the workshop area. When I say workshop it was more like an indoor stadium – the place was massive. Along the west wall, jacked high up off the floor on their own inboard hydraulic 'legs', sat the four gleaming racecars – completely stripped out. When I asked why they needed rebuilding, the race director said, 'Because of the immense strain placed on the cars driving them at their absolute limits all the time. 'So much wear and tear goes on with the engines, steering, drive trains and so on, that internal parts wear out very quickly, and others we replace simply to prevent them breaking down at a critical moment. 'But we don't replace these with just some cheap counterfeit parts one of our guys orders off the Internet – these are custom-made parts sourced from the race division of the factory in Germany – and they aren't cheap.'

So in my mind I'm starting to do the maths. The cars, the crew, the technology, the support trucks, the huge catering truck – complete with marquee, tables, chairs, chefs and waiting staff (yes, seriously) – and it's all looking like an awful lot of zeros before you even reach a decimal point.

But straightaway I could see a possible weakness in the plan. So much invested in everything else, yet the drivers were pretty much expected to turn up on the day in tip-top race condition.

But what if the driver – despite all the skills, talent, training, practice and coaching he might have from the team – turned up on race day in not such brilliant shape?

Suppose he'd had a meal the night before that didn't agree with him? What if he'd had an argument at home that morning and his mind wasn't on the job? What, say, he'd become unfit or dehydrated, or had an injury?

At the time when he straps himself into the car, that moment when man and machine become one, the total capacity for performance will ultimately be determined by the weakest element.

It doesn't matter to what degree the car has been prepared – if the driver isn't capable of performing to the same level, the potential to perform will never be realised.

There's a performance mismatch. An incongruence if you like. And when you have incongruence – when things aren't in alignment – you create conflict, stress and chaos.

And it would work the other way around too, wouldn't it? If you were to recruit one of the world's top racing drivers, and put them out on the track in my old mum's Morris Minor, you're really not going to expect anything like a 'competitive' result – are you?

> **Wealthy Body Wisdom:** *Running your life without energy is like running your business without money.*

Sure, he or she would wring the most that anybody could possibly get out of that car, but let's be honest: the total capacity for performance would ultimately be determined by the weakest element – in this case, the car.

And yet we see the same thing every day in business.

Most of our clients usually hold senior positions in their companies. The reason they earned those positions in the first place, and the reason they keep them, is their ability to perform at the sharp end of business. Their education, talent, skills, training, experience, competitive streak, intuition, leadership, expertise, quick-wittedness, drive – the list goes on.

But what do all these qualities have in common?

The answer is, they all happen from the neck up. It all goes on in their brains. Because that's what they're rewarded for. Very seldom is any consideration given to what's going on from the neck down.

Yet as human beings we're *not* disconnected at the neck. Otherwise we might as well just be a brain in a jar, plugged in somewhere to our laptops or iPhones, and that would be that.

No, our bodies are very much a part of everything we do and are. Like we said earlier, our brains are an organ of our body exactly the same as our heart, our liver, kidneys, lungs, skin – you name it. Understand this: the level of care we invest in our bodies from the neck down is the same level of care we're investing in our brains, and if that level doesn't match the same level of performance we expect from our brains every day, then that's a mismatch. An incongruence.

You see, a high-performance brain and a low-performance body don't match. A high-performance day and a low-performance breakfast don't match. A high-energy meeting supported by a low-energy body don't match.

They are incongruent. There's a performance mismatch. And when you have incongruence – when things aren't in alignment – you create internal conflict, stress and chaos.

This manifests itself in hyper-fatigue, headaches, low-grade aches and pains, weight gain, sexual dysfunction, chronic illness and eventually disease. Invest in your body at a high level – your brain is depending on it.

Wealthy Body Wisdom: So here's the thing to remember: your total capacity for performance will ultimately be determined by the weakest element. Anything you do from the neck up is totally dependent on everything you do from the neck down.

3.
NOBODY DIES OF OLD AGE

Dr Tom Mulholland is well known in New Zealand. An emergency room practitioner and an extreme sports enthusiast, he hosts his own show on radio and TV.

Known as the Attitude Doctor, his message is: *Live fast and die old.* Nobody ever dies of old age, he says; they die of disease. In fact, many people eat and drink themselves to a preventable early death because they ignore basic maintenance rules and symptoms.

And dying isn't pretty. There's more to it than just the pain and stress of being rushed to hospital on a stretcher. Dr Mulholland says that he sees grown men, suffering from acute heart attacks, cry for their mothers or suddenly start to pray – not wanting to die.

He sees women wanting to see their children one more time or desperately mourning for the things they hadn't yet achieved.

And the sad fact is most of what he sees in the emergency room is preventable. Here are some of the many mistaken beliefs and attitudes we come across on a daily basis:

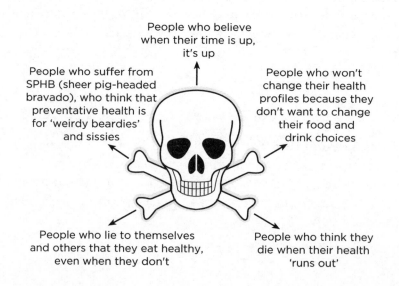

People who believe when their time is up, it's up

People who suffer from SPHB (sheer pig-headed bravado), who think that preventative health is for 'weirdy beardies' and sissies

People who won't change their health profiles because they don't want to change their food and drink choices

People who lie to themselves and others that they eat healthy, even when they don't

People who think they die when their health 'runs out'

The various alarms that the human body uses to alert itself to danger are ignored, overruled or interpreted as mere signs of ageing. Such cues include:

- » fatigue
- » poor sleep
- » lack of concentration
- » depression
- » aches and pains
- » shortness of breath
- » weight gain

These are all messages alerting you to the need for change.

But you shouldn't just be waiting for alerts. You should be monitoring yourself too, and making sure you are in as good condition as you can be. The information you need includes the following:

- » Blood pressure – should be around 120/80
- » Cholesterol – should be around 5.2 total, or 200mg/dl, and adjusted for age
- » Homocysteine – should be below 10, but 5 is optimal; find out more on page 102
- » Blood glucose – should be between 4–8mml/l
- » Waist circumference – should be less than 96cm (38 inches) for men, 76cm (30 inches) for women
- » Resting heart rate – should be around 70 bpm or lower depending on fitness
- » Moles and skin – abnormalities should be investigated
- » Hormone balances – a full endocrine panel, including DHEA and cortisol

All this should be reviewed regularly and enthusiastically.
Yes, that is what we said: *enthusiastically.*
So make an appointment right now for a health check. Get all these results and get to know your own numbers. Do it *now.*

Wealthy Body Action Point: *It is essential that you keep track of your personal metabolic numbers and data, and remain alert for change.*

You need to understand that diseases are not just things you catch, or that just show up as the random finger of fate. Instead, they are related directly to your environment, your diet and your lifestyle.

The traditional way of thinking about health and ageing is outdated, and will not help us address the plethora of illnesses and diseases that may conspire to prevent a wealthy body from reaching its full potential.

We evolved in a world without fast-food outlets, supermarkets or convenience coffee shops on every corner. We didn't have to contend with battery-farmed animals, artificial growth hormones, antibiotics, GM foods or the proliferation of high sugar, refined oils and denatured-fat foods.

The threat now is not the sabre-toothed tiger; it is our own ecosystem and the modern environment we have created.

The key to smart survival now lies in understanding how you work, to ensure that your internal orchestra is playing in tune and enable you to navigate our increasingly toxic environment.

It is no good just thinking that a problem with one part of your body is an isolated case, unconnected to other parts – too often, the premise of today's medical 'sick-care' system. No good either, relying on a drug (or series of drugs) to fix the problem without considering, or even knowing, the impact on the whole body.

You are *not* a collection of unrelated parts. You have to take responsibility for your survival and think 'health-care' and 'self-care' for optimal performance and longevity.

> **Wealthy Body Wisdom:** *Aim to die young – but very, very old.*

Advertising Will Kill You

Your body is trying hard to tell you what you need to know. Your body has a dashboard, a GPS that delivers all types of essential information. Yet it is drowned out by advertising. All adverts have two things in common. First they promote an ideal and make viewers feel bad or inadequate for not attaining it. Then they promise an easy, effort-free way to try to attain that ideal. Cold medication adverts, for example, make it appear that it is wrong to have a cold, even though successful transition through a cold actually bolsters the immune system. Eye-drop adverts tell viewers it is bad to have bloodshot eyes, even when that redness comes from the body's own techniques for healing and replenishing damage within the eye. And, of course, every prepared food manufacturer out there speaks to the value of satisfying hunger while ignoring the value of nutrition.

As we said in the first chapter, you live in a body that hasn't caught up with the times. Advertisers promise you health and salvation and their products on the shelves seem to offer a fast, easy, effort-free solution.

And sadly, the true guardians of health – such as dark-coloured vegetables, unprocessed foods, exercise and balance – are lost in a sea of light and sound. Your 50,000-year-old innocent but loyal body has been deposited smack in the middle of Piccadilly Circus, or Times Square, with no clue how to escape.

The upshot of all this is that too many of us have been conditioned to believe that because illness is bad, anything pertaining to illness is bad, including the body's own attempts to repair itself. Denial, it seems, is more comfortable than confrontation. And preventative measures such as diet and exercise, are too difficult.

Why is All the Fun Food Bad For Me?

Our taste buds have been led astray; they were designed for a different time and a different environment. Most of what tasted good to our ancestors, tasted good because it was good for them.

Go back in time, and we find that humans were eating literally no grains or sugars. Today, the bulk of the food that most people eat is based on grains or sugar.

Food-processing methods have also changed. The foods we eat now are very different from the foods that humans have traditionally eaten – yet our bodies are the same.

Over the years, food companies have studied, in minute detail, our every eating habit and taste preference and discovered what stimulates our taste and desire to over-eat. Sugar, salt and fat have been at the forefront of this change.

The food giants have added them to nutritionally cheap foods, meaning that they now taste good – to the point that they can become addictive. However, they do little to satisfy the body's needs.

Your body keeps craving the nutrients that are supposed to come down that long digestive tube of yours along with all this sugar, salt, fat and flavour enhancers. Trouble is, they never arrive!

Have you ever considered how much everyday advertising deals with food or food-like substances, manipulating us to buy them?

Wealthy Body Wisdom: What are NDFs?

NDFs refer to the difference between eating nutrient-deficient foods (high calorie, low nutrition) and nutrient-dense foods (high nutrition, lower calorie).

NDFs, or nutrient-dense foods, have a lot to compete with as habits and taste buds have been corrupted.

It's a bit like drinking cola, compared to drinking water; if you are used to drinking cola, then water tastes bland. This is why we think vegetables or unsweetened foods are tasteless. Our taste buds have become used to an explosion of taste; when we eat normal foods, they taste bland.

This is partly why we now have a global obesity epidemic.

Investing in a good spice rack and some new food choices can make a huge difference. The more you adapt to a natural way of eating, the more these fresh foods come alive. There are many fantastic alternatives to ice cream, chocolate, alcohol and takeaways. It is like giving up sugar in tea or cola drinks; once you have stopped, you wonder how you ever tolerated them.

For example, coconut sugar is an alternative to refined white sugar that opens up a whole world of recipe opportunities.

So how is coconut sugar healthier than white sugar? Well, its key advantage is it's packed with nutrition. While white sugar is stripped of nutrients due to processing, coconut sugar retains its rich mineral content,

---

including calcium, iron, zinc and potassium, due to minimal processing. Coconut sugar originates from the flowers of the coconut palm. The sap from the flower buds is collected and heated until the moisture evaporates leaving a thick paste, which solidifies and is ground into granules.

Coconut sugar also creates less havoc with your blood sugar levels. This is due to coconut sugar's low glycaemic index (GI) rating – a measure which tests how quickly a food raises your blood sugar level. The lower the better, so your blood sugar level remains stable and isn't 'spiked' by certain foods.

The more NDFs you eat, the more your cravings subside and you begin to hunger for what your body really needs, instead of what the food manufacturers want you to crave. Now everything you desire will be good for you, and you always have the opportunity to let off some steam and treat yourself at occasional social outings!

Wealthy Body Action Points

1. Fake it 'til you make it. *Eat NDFs first. Then – and only then – see if you still want to indulge. Remember: 'He who stuffeth, puffeth!'*

2. Get used to the idea that to get what you want, some things are going to be boring. It comes under the heading of grooming and body maintenance, like having to get a haircut, cleaning your teeth or having to shave.

Enthusiasm Will Keep You Alive Longer

The trick to developing The Wealthy Body and to keep it functioning in the long term is to change the conditioned attitude about the aches, pains and worries related to illness, and embrace them enthusiastically; to recognise and rejoice in the fact that the human body can actually talk to its owner; that the messages provide guidance or requests, and that there is a great deal of healing, maintenance and growth that can be achieved, both reactively (through listening to these messages) and proactively by changing your habits.

Wealthy Body Wisdom: Get to grips with your body early. Diseases often take years to manifest themselves.

The Four Stages of Health

Experts now agree that, metabolically speaking, most people live quite well until the age of 25 or so, after which they start to disintegrate. Most degenerative diseases start around 25 to 35 years of age, at a point where we still consider ourselves to be invincible and possibly immortal. From that point, we seem to rush headlong into an epidemic of frailty, obesity, infertility and mental collapse.

Out of the Four Stages of Health listed below, we know that, unfortunately, the majority of the population exists in Stages 1 and 2. The result is bodies propped up on little else other than medication, denial and hope.

Check and rate yourself on the following 4-stage assessment:

Stage 1: Slowly Drowning (requires no effort)
You're not going to make it...

» sickness/headaches from bad diet, caffeine and alcohol damage, plus no exercise
» chronic fatigue from poor sleep, dehydration, vitamin and mineral deficiency – meaning that you wake up more tired than when you went to bed
» low threshold to sickness from collapsed immunity, and heavy reliance on medication
» difficulty making it through the day from low energy and poor resilience

» difficulty concentrating
» numerous days off from feelings of hopelessness, frustration, depression

Stage 2: Just Keeping Head Above Water (requires some effort)

You might just get by…

» occasional sickness, risk of disease from struggling immunity; taking medications 'as required'
» just enough, but no spare energy. You eat better, relying on snacking for energy, and your sleeping is OK but not restful
» only just making it through the day, exercising occasionally, but needing weekends to recover

Stage 3: Swimming Strongly (requires consistent and conscientious effort)

You're going to make it OK…

» getting through the day without difficulty. You are more confident, clear-headed, positive
» the energy and fitness to pursue leisure activities; a healthier and more balanced diet; and sound sleep, leading to better energy levels and resilience
» maintaining healthy body shape and composition, so reducing risk of disease. Exercising 2–3 times per week, and body-conscious
» fewer instances of illness/fatigue/aches and pains. No need for stimulants, sugar or drugs to get through the working day

Stage 4: Running on Dry Land (requires discipline, commitment, regularity, smart thinking)

The optimal level of existence…

» high level of activity possible. You are strong, fit and dynamic, exercising hard most days
» great body shape and composition. You are lean, hard, tough and supremely confident – and have the lowest risk of degenerative diseases, collapsing posture, aches and pains

» boosted energy and mood levels. You are animated, alert and on top of your game with optimal nutrition and business 'drive' hormones (the hormones that are responsible for mood, drive and focus)

» instances of illness are rare. Your immunity is strong, and risk of disease minimal

» high levels of enjoyment of life – and the ability to seek new challenges, and triumph

Stage 4 represents Excellent Health and is attainable at any age. Yes, it requires consistent and mindful work to maintain – but the rewards are huge! *Which stage are YOU?*

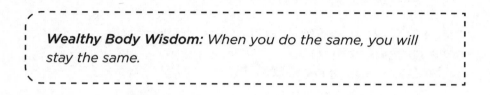

Wealthy Body Wisdom: *When you do the same, you will stay the same.*

4.
FOOD: YOU ARE WHAT YOU EAT, SO EAT BETTER

Come on – this isn't rocket science. Or is it? The human body is one of the most incredibly complex, yet marvellously capable, organisms on the planet. So is it any wonder that we struggle to look after it? But think about this: rocket science isn't complicated for a rocket scientist. Flying a jumbo jet isn't difficult for a jumbo jet pilot. Therefore, being a human being shouldn't be difficult for a human being. You are one. You have an obligation to sit down and learn how you work, how you function and how to maintain yourself to keep running at your peak and potential as you age.

And this is where we start.

Your body is a superhighway of sophisticated activity. It processes approximately one billion messages per second, pumping blood on its journey through 100,000km (62,000 miles) of arteries, capillaries and veins per day. Every second it is constantly destroying and replacing millions of cells – skin, liver, stomach, skeleton, brain cells, etc.

More than 98 per cent of the cells of your body, including muscles, organs and bones, are replaced every year. Fifty thousand cells in your body will have died and been replaced with new cells by the time you have finished reading this page. This miracle all happens as we deal with a multitude of other daily activities.

Across developed nations we spend 70 per cent of health budgets on dealing with preventable diseases. Spending it on prevention first would be wiser!

> *Wealthy Body Wisdom:* It takes only three days for your cells to change and your body to come back to life after changing your diet for the better.

Losing Weight with Food

Have you ever wondered how actors get their weight down quickly for a specific role or how bodybuilders get their body fat so low it shows off all their muscle structure? Here's how they do it:

Achieving a lean body and looking great is simply a matter of knowing exactly what to eat, when to eat it, and how much to eat, combined with the proper training programme.

As the old saying goes, *Everything is difficult before it becomes easy.* And we know from personal experience that eating right can be perplexing.

When you eat the correct foods, the volume of food in your daily diet increases. Unrefined natural foods are typically bulkier and contain fewer calories, ounce per ounce, than refined processed foods.

When you eat unrefined foods, you feel full on fewer calories. Therefore you have to eat more (quantity) and more frequently.

Despite all the current fad diet regimes, we still recommend four to five small meals spaced throughout the day. Eating this way is one of the key secrets to staying in shape. This multiple-meal technique provides the maximum benefit for stimulating the metabolism and feeding nutrients to that all-important, fat-burning furnace: lean muscle tissue.

Many people ask, 'How in the world can I eat so many times per day? I'm just not hungry in the morning ... I normally skip breakfast and I don't eat much during the day.'

> *Wealthy Body Wisdom:* Don't snack between meals – eat a meal between meals!

Want to get FAT? Do this...

Some people skip meals, opting to save their calories for a heavy dinner. This is a practice that guarantees an overweight body. Your metabolism simply cannot effectively utilise the number of calories that you have consumed in just two meals or less. Excess calories are immediately deposited as fat. Additionally, your metabolism is not stimulated sufficiently by just two feedings per day. Nor is muscle tissue adequately fed with just two meals per day. Consequently, your metabolism ends up so much lower than it has to be.

Want to get FIT? Do this...

Getting used to four or five small meals per day need not be difficult. View your daily diet as three square meals per day – breakfast, lunch and dinner – with a small meal in-between breakfast and lunch, and another between lunch and dinner. If you have a late evening, another small snack after dinner gets you to a total of six small meals for the day.

The trick is to begin the day with a small meal, so that you get hungry two to three hours later. You then have another small meal or snack. Then two to three hours later, you have lunch. And so forth. By deliberately keeping the amounts of food small, you get hungry frequently – and this is exactly what you want.

By eating small meals throughout the day, you keep from overloading your body with too many calories at one time. Hence, there is less excess available for deposition as fat.

If you're one of those people who do not eat breakfast and cannot imagine eating anything in the morning or afternoon because you have no appetite, try this:

» Skip your dinner one evening. By skipping dinner, you will go to bed hungrier and the next morning you will be quite ravenous.
» Resist the urge to gorge, and eat a small breakfast.
» Stay hungry. Two to three hours later, have your next small meal.
» Two to three hours later, have your lunch and so forth as above.

Keep the meals small on purpose until you get the hang of just how much you can eat during each meal so that you still get hungry before the next meal.

Once you get used to eating these small meals periodically during the day, your metabolism will really speed up because of the constant processing of food.

This is calorie-burning without effort! And it will, in turn, lead to a larger appetite. Yet here's where the paradox kicks in. Up to a certain point, and as long as you're eating the correct foods, the more you eat more frequently, the faster your metabolism will work. If you eat junk, though, you will simply get fat.

By eating the correct foods in the correct amounts frequently throughout the day, you will master the ability to speed up your metabolism to achieve the lean body that you've always strived for, no matter what your age.

Wealthy Body Action Points

1. Plan your meals like you plan your meetings. Go into your day knowing where and what you'll be eating, and at what time. You wouldn't leave business decisions to chance, so don't leave your nutrition to chance.

2. If buying your lunch, buy a second portion at the same time for your meal mid-afternoon (4 p.m.).

3. Avoid hunger.

Eat in Order to Meet

A number of years ago, while working with an executive team, I was approached by the company CEO, Richard, who said, 'Tim, I'd like to join the programme.'

This was, of course, great news, but to be honest I wasn't immediately sure what result he was personally interested in achieving. He was a competitive sportsman, extremely fit, had a healthy diet, didn't drink and seemed to be in overall terrific shape.

When I asked him about this, he replied, 'Well, I've noticed a number of changes in the men and women you're already working with in my team – some are getting fitter, some are losing weight and others are adopting much healthier lifestyle habits around exercise, coffee, food and alcohol. But the biggest difference I see is how much more energy they have. It's like they're different people. They come into the office bursting with energy, they're stepping off long-haul flights sharp and alert, and firing on all cylinders, all day long – and I'd like a piece of that.'

'Really? So are energy levels a problem for you right now?' I asked.

He said, 'Let me give you an example: yesterday in an important meeting, I dozed off to sleep.'

I said, 'Was that a major issue?'

'You don't understand,' he said. 'I was taking it.'

So here was a fit, driven and dynamic Chief Executive, literally dropping into a coma in the middle of a meeting, in the middle of the afternoon. What gives?

Turns out he'd made a mistake that we see many others make every day. He had no awareness of his daily nutrient intake.

When you're a person who works out every day, who plays sports all the time and who never sits still in the same place for long, you need to be really strategic about fuelling your body.

Just eating fruit for breakfast, skipping lunch and eating late for dinner, isn't going to be enough to sustain your energy levels through a busy high-flying day. It just isn't.

It doesn't make sense, and your body knows that. It can't verbalise the problem to you, so instead it does the next best thing: it shuts down.

To maintain your health and energy levels, you have to keep track of what you do, what you eat and who you are. It's a full-time job, but the results are immediate and very tangible.

I'm Hungry! I'm Being Cued to Eat

Are you being cued to eat?

The stimulating effects of food have the power to make you act without conscious awareness and often against your better judgement. The reward centres of the brain become stimulated. We often react to forces we do not recognise.

After decades of trying to unravel the mystery of why people struggle with energy, brain fog, depression, body fat and self-esteem, the one crucial element we have always come back to has been the brain.

Our ancient brains are being influenced through the smoke and mirror tactics of the food industry. We are being manipulated on a grand scale, as marketing tugs on our primal survival instincts in order to trigger us to buy more and more of their products. This happens through the highly profitable manufacturing and marketing model that makes foods layered in processed grains, denatured oils, sugar and salt widely available.

We have also been conditioned, often through advertising, to associate these foods with positive emotions and with environments that foster these associations.

What you eat and drink today is how you will feel, think and look tomorrow. So, to ensure we retain the ability to choose the healthiest options for our needs, we must constantly investigate, challenge and unravel the cues and information we receive from the sophisticated marketing, packaging and advertising of our foods.

Every time we resist the desire for foods loaded with sugar, fat and salt, it makes it easier to act differently – and break the cycle of cue–urge–reward–habit which lies at the core of poor health and weight gain.

Protect Yourself

» Eat more healthy fats from eggs, avocados, coconut oil, nuts and seeds.

» Eat a large variety of organic coloured vegetables and fruits. Aim for 8–9 servings of fresh vegetables (a serving is about a teacup size) plus 2–3 servings of fruit daily.

» Eat only meat from an animal that has had a fit, free-range, healthy life. This encourages a higher level of omega-3 as well as vitamins and minerals.

» Eat only foods that look like foods. For example, a carrot looks like a carrot – but carrot cake doesn't. Carrot cake might contain some carrot but it is largely made from refined flour and sugar – and, if shop-bought, flavourings, stabilisers, preservatives and hydrogenated oils. This complicated mixture guarantees taste, stability, texture and visual pleasure, but it does nothing good for the body and brain. In fact, it can do a lot of harm.

» Eat greens, not grains. To reduce inflammation in the body and improve immunity, include regular portions of brassicas, such as cabbage, kale, broccoli, cauliflower and Brussels sprouts. They are high in antioxidants, which specifically help protect against some cancers, especially lung, stomach and colon cancer.

» Cut the refined oestrogenic foods out of your diet, such as wheat and unfermented soy. Soy milk and tofu are both high in phytoestrogens, goitrogens (thyroid suppressors) and phytic acid.

Vegetables? I Hated Them as a Kid and I Hate Them Now!

Think about this for a moment. Why do people hate vegetables so much? The answer to this question reveals a great deal about why we are at the unhealthy place we are currently in, and how we can easily get out of it.

Kids don't like vegetables because they taste plain and are hard and crunchy. Kids have an aversion to plain tastes and tougher textures, which is why so many of them also want the crusts cut off their bread.

Kids seek out sweet tastes because our ancient metabolisms – which are still stuck 100,000 years in the past, long before the invention of the chocolate bar – understand sweet to be located in fruits and wild honey, both of which contain the vitamins and antioxidants essential for building immunity in children. High colour equals high potency, and fruits are usually brightly coloured – red, yellow, blue, orange and green. Think about that for a moment.

Children's aversion to plain tastes, along with their attraction to sweet tastes and bright colours, have been exploited for years by the makers of breakfast cereals. Colours on the packaging always include red, yellow, blue, orange and green, as well as large eyes on the characters, to which children are also instinctively drawn. These cereal boxes are then placed mid-height on supermarket shelves, precisely at eye-level for small children riding in the shopping trollies. They see, they want, they reach – and they cry if they do not get it.

This is just one example of the ways in which food companies exploit our ancient instincts. Vegetables are another. Because you probably did not like vegetables as a child – especially if you were allowed to opt for sugary cereals, treats and desserts instead – this experience during your formative years is carried through, reinforced and magnified in your adult years. If as much money was spent making broccoli as sexy and attractive as Coca-Cola, a lot more people would happily eat broccoli.

As it is, our bodies are left to fend for themselves, and consequently they always lose.

Remember, Coca-Cola will still be in business long after you are dead.

Ultimately, your body can learn (or re-learn) to love the good food you put into it. Marketers do not always have to win.

Enzymes and Cooking

In our earlier years, we did not cook our food to death. Only in the period since the end of World War II has the convenience of fast-cooking and over-cooking become predominant. We call it *cooking to death*, because that's what happens to food when you cook it. The valuable enzymes from which we draw nutrition are damaged by over-cooking and over-processing.

> *High blood pressure can affect children as young as four.*

Cooking makes food safer, certainly. Our goal here is not to eliminate cooking from our lives – but there is a gulf between cooking a food, and heating it. Heating food kills the bacteria that can do harm. That's good. Over-cooking, however, kills almost everything else, including the all-important enzymes. That's not so good.

Once food reaches 47.5°C (118°F), many of the enzymes required for maintaining good health are killed. A recent study by the Mayo Clinic consequently showed that 70 per cent of us have to turn to at least one pharmaceutical drug or other to patch up the damage.

Your body cannot manufacture enzymes on its own; they have to come from good quality, high-protein foods. Enzymes can be damaged by high temperatures or extremes of pH (acid OR alkaline (caustic)). Amino acids can be found in all food sources, including animal and plant foods, some having more concentrated yields than others. When poor-quality food is provided instead, the result is poor digestion, tiredness and lethargy, which makes you reach for the nearest caffeine-and-quick-sugar-pick-me-up – in the mistaken belief that caffeine will help.

Even though caffeine is a stimulant, the result is often more fatigue, because you haven't taken on board any vitamins, nutrients, minerals, calories or enzymes to fuel the body at a cellular level. Plus it costs the body more energy trying to break down the pollutants and additives found in the quick snack foods that often go with that afternoon cappuccino. This overwhelms the body further, leading to mood swings, brain fog, food intolerances, yeast infections, poor memory and niggling injuries. All are side effects to the lack of nutrients and enzymes.

Your system cannot detoxify your body without healthy enzymes.

Myth: Microwave ovens are a healthy way to cook food.

A: Research demonstrates that there is a loss of nutrition in food that has been microwaved. A study published in the November 2003 issue of The Journal of the Science of Food and Agriculture *found that broccoli 'zapped' in the microwave with a little water lost up to 97 per cent of its beneficial antioxidants. By comparison, steamed broccoli lost 11 per cent – or less. There were also reductions in phenolic compounds and glucosinolates, but mineral levels remained intact.*

There is also a strong school of thought that the microwaves in these ovens damage cell walls of foods to a degree that the gut receptors find it difficult to recognise the particles as food. This results in an immune response failure over time.

Foods That Cause Disease

Everything you enjoy is bad for you. You've probably heard that expression, and you have probably uttered it yourself. It's true. Almost everything you like is bad for you. But think: why do you like these things? It is likely because you have been told to like them through the marvellous machinery of marketing.

For example, if you love a particular brand of biscuit, it is probably not because you are in love with hydrogenated palm oil and dextromethorphan. It is probably because the aroma, taste and texture of this product brings back pleasant memories, or provides a moment of relaxation or even indulgence. It's an association that generates an addiction that generates sales.

So yes, most of the things you like are bad for you. But the good news, once again, is that your body can easily learn to like new things. And once that happens, all the things you like then become good for you.

Wealthy Body Wisdom: The only way to keep your health is to eat what you don't want, drink what you don't like, and do what you'd rather not.

> *Wealthy Body Wisdom: The greatest threat to the corporate bottom line, is employees who simply can't be bothered looking after themselves better...*

Now, don't freak out. Do us a favour. Read this next part – and do not despair. We have answers for you. You will not have to face a life of eating lichen and grubs – that's a promise. Here are seven things you're probably eating too much of that are bad for you.

(It's probably also time for 20 more push-ups, don't you think?)

Processed Grains Are Bad For You

Cereal grains were introduced into mankind's food supply only about 10,000 years ago. Prior to this, cereal of any kind was rare. Today's processed cereal grains not only rob our diet of vitamins, minerals and fibre, but they also change our mix of macronutrients (carbohydrates, proteins, fats), by adding a grain carbohydrate load for which our metabolism is still not prepared.

> *Wealthy Body Action Point: Instead of toast, cereals and croissants for breakfast, start the day on unprocessed whole foods instead. Try quinoa, a seed that's high in protein, omega-3 and multi-vitamins. Alternatively, go for a boiled egg or omelette, or try a vegetable-based smoothie as an easy, fast option.*

Processed Meats Are Bad For You

The second big change in our food, between 8,000 and 5,000 years ago, was the domestication of animals. This introduced us to dairy foods and cultivated meat, which were rare or non-existent in our ancient diet.

Meat from wild game animals is always lean, healthy and organic, but farmed animals became more sedentary, over-fed and less healthy.

More recently, processed cheeses, margarines, and meat products changed the composition of our nutrient and fat intake, by adding large amounts of trans-fats, preservatives, stabilisers, flavourings, colourings and chemicals.

Wealthy Body Action Point: When choosing meats, opt for organically raised, grass-fed, free-range animals, which have a higher content of omega fats. They also tend to be leaner, as well as free from traces of agrochemicals and animal drugs. Select cold cuts that look like the meat you'd expect to see: sliced ham off the bone looks very different to the pre-formed 'mystery food' that passes for ham in packets.

Sugar is Bad For You

The third big change was sugar, which used to come to us in the form of limited amounts of natural honey, as well as the sugars found in seasonal fruits and berries. Sugar was a minor item in our pre-agricultural diet, and refined sugars were non-existent. Some 250 years ago, our intake was around 1.8kg (4lb) per person per year, whereas now the average consumption is closer to 64.4kg (142lb) a year. Our DNA hasn't changed one bit, but our diets certainly have! Refined sugar, and its 1970s progeny high-fructose corn syrup (HFCS), has also pushed our glycaemic load into dangerous overdrive.

Our consumption of HFCS has increased by 387 per cent since 1970. HFCS is highly processed and, unlike table sugar, its fructose and glucose molecules are not chemically bound, opening the pathway for excessive load on the liver and insulin system at the same time. Excessive amounts of any sugar in the diet has toxic effects, and processed fructose is far worse, from a metabolic standpoint, than refined sugar.

Female mice fed a diet that contained 25 per cent of calories from corn syrup had nearly twice the death rate compared to those fed a diet in which 25 per cent of calories came from table sugar.

Moreover, mice fed corn syrup also had 26 per cent fewer offspring than their sugar-fed counterparts...

Wealthy Body Action Point: Always check the label of foods you buy in packets. If the sugar value represents more than 25 per cent of the total carbohydrates – leave it on the shelf.

Salt is Very Bad For You

The fourth change was salt (sodium). Except for occasional ingestion of seaweed and saltwater, human salt consumption was relatively low. Today, however, more than 80 per cent of the salt we eat has been added to food, and we expect it. Unsalted food now tastes bland. Added salt does a real number on us by reversing the sodium-potassium ratio (Na-K ratio) – from low-sodium/high-potassium as we enjoyed in our ancient unprocessed diet, to high-sodium/low-potassium that we experience now. Our kidney function and blood pressure are genetically programmed for the older, original low-sodium/high-potassium diet.

Potassium levels are naturally high in vegetables and fruits, and sodium levels are naturally low. Large amounts of sodium are often added to foods during processing. So choosing produce that is fresh or frozen, or choosing foods that have not had salt added in processing, can help curb dietary sodium and boost potassium.

Currently, food labelling does not require the potassium content of foods to be listed. But often foods that are highest in potassium are those that don't carry a label. Good sources include vegetables and fruits, especially leafy green vegetables, such as spinach and collards; orange vegetables, such as sweet potato, pumpkin and squash; citrus fruits, such as oranges and grapefruits; and dried beans.

Consuming a diet with a high ratio of potassium helps improve digestion, muscle function and bone health, and lowers risk of hypertension (high blood pressure), heart disease and stroke.

To spice up the flavour of your meals, you could try adding a slice or squeeze of lemon, sliced garlic, spring onion, lemon or lime zest, matchsticks of ginger or slices of chilli. You could also add a side of hummus, chutney or relish, or drizzle a little balsamic vinegar over your salad.

If you do add seasoning to your food, we recommend you choose Himalayan salt, which has spent thousands of years maturing under tectonic pressure, locked far away from the pollutants, heavy metals and industrial toxins now present in our seawater. It also contains less sodium than table salt, and retains more than 80 trace minerals that are important for cellular balance in our bodies, including magnesium and potassium.

Most Vegetable Oils Are Bad For You

The fifth change in our food was the introduction of processed vegetable oils, another non-existent item in nature. As we progressed technologically, these fats became more and more artificial. Now most processed vegetable oils are high in trans-fatty acids, and some have added colouring, which is even worse for your health.

Trans-fatty acids are liquid fats that have been hydrogenated or partially hydrogenated to make them more solid at room temperature. This happens by blasting the natural fats with hydrogen in an industrial process (to turn oil into margarine, for example), or when some oils and fats are superheated (when frying at high temperature, for example). In the United States, the Food & Drug Administration has introduced new labelling laws that require manufacturers to list the trans-fat content of their products. In response, many companies advertise that their products are free of trans-fats. What they don't tell you is they've substituted palm oil, which promotes heart disease almost as much as trans-fats do. Hundreds of studies show a link between heart disease and consumption of hydrogenated oils. An editorial in *The New York Times* in June 2015 highlighted a ruling from the FDA that requires food manufacturers to eliminate trans-fats from all foods by 2018.

Wealthy Body Action Point: *Don't cook with liquid oils. Instead use coconut oil or organic butter, which are* solid *at room temperature, as they won't convert to trans-fats so readily when heated. Keep other high-quality oils, like extra-virgin olive oil, for* lightly *drizzling cold on salads, and store in a cool, dark place in your kitchen, which will help prolong their life and prevent them going rancid. Use olive oil sparingly and, if you really like the taste of olive in your food, eat olives instead.*

Myth: *I like margarine – is it better for me than butter?*

A: *If man-made it, don't eat it! Avoid foods that pretend to be something they are not, they are not good for you. Nature doesn't like margarine: if you leave it out in the garden, insects won't touch it, animals won't go near it, and even bacteria won't break it down. Get used to not eating spreads by default.*

Fibre is Good For You, But You Don't Get Any, Which is Bad For You

Our great-great-great forebears of thousands of years ago enjoyed about 100g (3½oz) per day of fibre. It came in many forms – from roots, fruits, nuts and vegetables. Today's current severe processing of carbohydrates and vegetables removes most of the fibre, because frankly, fibre is indigestible and therefore hard to deal with. But that's precisely why we need it: to clean out the system from top to bottom (literally) and to eliminate pollutants and carcinogens. Now we are lucky to get 20g (¾oz) of fibre a day, and from a very narrow range of sources. So guess what? Manufacturers sell it back to us in the form of packaged bran, usually on the grocery shelf.

Wealthy Body Action Point: Get whole fresh fibre from eating more vegetables – especially broccoli, cabbage, cauliflower, berries, beans and lettuce. Have green smoothies instead of juices, and occasional dates and figs (careful!). Drink lots of water to keep fibre moving smoothly through your digestive system, otherwise it can compact and dry out in your bowel.

Wealthy Body Wisdom: A person who eats a typical diet of refined foods holds approximately eight undigested meals' worth of waste in their intestine. A person who eats a high-fibre diet typically holds approximately three undigested meals...

Micronutrients Are Good For You, But You Don't Get Many of These Either

There has been a systematic reduction or removal of vitamins, minerals and polyphenols (plant phenols and plant sterols, or oils) in the majority of our commonly available foods. Sometimes this is due to over-processing and sometimes to soil degradation – remember when soil used to be dark, rich, moist and heavy? Now, through loss of humus material from intensive farming and the over-use of chemicals, it's more likely to be light, sandy-textured and dry. With the exception of sodium, the vitamin and mineral intake in our ancient diet was up to eight times what it is now.

Now at this point you might wonder why food companies go to all these lengths to strip our food of nutrients. After all, is that not counterproductive? Not when the company that makes the food also makes the medicines to compensate for the poor food. Be aware too that much of the health information we receive on packaging and in the media is driven by the manufacturers themselves.

Besides, nutrients and all the other good things that go into food are very fragile. They are not designed to sit in boxes for days or weeks. They are designed to be consumed now. And if you don't consume them, other organisms will. That's why good food spoils. And the last thing a commercial food provider wants is rotting food on display. So it's best to strip the food of all that nature needs to encourage spoilage. The rest is the customer's problem.

Wealthy Body Action Point: *Avoid products that claim they can lower your cholesterol because they contain polyphenols (plant phenols and plant sterols). Plant phenols and sterols can indeed help lower cholesterol, but if you want high-quality plant polyphenols, guess what? Plants contain plant polyphenols – eat more of them instead!*

Acidity is Bad For You

Our ancestors ate a basically alkaline diet of unprocessed foods. The modern environment– cereal grains, processed carbohydrates, dairy foods; high levels of salt, sugar, sodas; processed vegetable oils; alcohol; and very low levels of micronutrients and fibre – overwhelms our genetically programmed mechanisms that regulate acid/alkaline balance. Now our bodies are far more acidic.

Want proof? Acid reflux disease and indigestion disorders that are mostly preventable fuel a $7 billion industry in the United States alone. Many of the causes of acid reflux disease, gout, gastro-oesophageal reflux disease (GURD) and others are directly linked to a high-acid diet.

Wealthy Body Action Point: Aim to eat more alkalising foods in your diet. Weirdly enough, lemons are highly alkalising as are most vegetables – especially greens, beetroot and brassicas. Avocado, almonds and herbal teas also help balance against high-acid foods. It's all about balancing acid/alkaline foods on your plate before you eat them, so if you eat 1 serving of meat (high acid) make sure you eat 3 servings of vegetables to balance it out.

Other high-acid foods include bread, rice and pasta, which are largely nutrient deficient and should probably be avoided anyway. Surprisingly enough, many healthy foods are also high acid – there is nothing wrong with that and they should not be avoided as they are essential to good health, so it's simply a case of balancing them out. These include certain nuts (walnuts, pistachios, cashews, Brazils and peanuts), as well as mustard, ketchup and mayonnaise. High-alkaline foods you can use to help balance out include almonds (so mixed nuts may be perfectly fine), potatoes and egg whites. Egg whites are alkaline but egg yolks are high acid, and their overall rating is slightly on the acid side.

All these factors are costly to your physical and mental health. Failure to redress these relatively modern dietary anomalies, and return to a healthier, unprocessed and unadulterated diet, may spawn a myriad of different illnesses and disease, including many cancers, motor neurone disease, diabetes and dementia.

Yet incredibly, to any high achiever, illness may not be the worst effect. The worst effect of the nutritionally restricted expression of your ancestral DNA is that you will never be able to build that body with which you can reach your full potential. And the saddest part about this is that you will not even know, because your brain will also be fed poorly, so that you cannot even perceive the potential you may have.

Your food choices are vital building components to the structure of your brain, your muscles, your organs, your emotions, your genes, your immune system, your energy, your hormones, how you see, how you look and how you perform.

> *Life is too short to go around in an unhealthy body. A great physique is not a matter of chance but a matter of choice!*

Evolution and Longer Lives

Many times when we deliver this litany of bad nutritional news to our clients, we get some good questions back. One of these is, '*Why can we not simply evolve to handle modern foods?*' The answer is that adaptation and significant changes could occur over hundreds of thousands – and maybe millions – of years. The changes in the way we find, create, process and consume food have come along within only a few generations, far too quick a time for our genetics to take notice.

A second objection to what we talk about is the fact that more people are living longer today than they were a century and more ago. There is far less chance that you will be eaten by a sabre-tooth tiger on your way to Starbucks, or even that you will be struck down by polio before the weekend.

Indeed, science has gone a long way towards eliminating a vast number of sources of early death, at least in the developed world. But we then spend much of those won-back years spending billions on drugs, medicines and other reactive cures. Sadly, there's just too much money to be made in keeping people alive and unhealthy, than in teaching people how to *be* alive and healthy.

For Crying Out Loud, What Else is There to Eat?

So finally, what is there to eat? Well, a lot, actually. Most grocery stores offer organic products, free-range meats and preservative-free foods. They are a little more expensive, because they cost more to raise and transport than processed foods, but the good news is, you don't need to consume as much, so you actually come out ahead. You save money at the till by not buying all the processed, dead, unhealthy foods that you used to eat and drink and at the other end in health costs.

Change your shopping list, and change your approach. More meals, but fewer calories. More nutrition and less poison.

Diet Soft Drinks

When a person consumes an artificial sweetener, the brain senses it is eating something sweet and so it expects calories and nutrients. But neither show up.

When people consume beverages without calories and without feeling full, this stimulates the brain to want to eat more, which magnifies the craving for sugar.

Artificial sweeteners are often super-sweet. For example, both acesulfame K (also known as Sunett, Sweet One and Sweet & Safe) and aspartame (Nutrasweet, Equal, Sugar Twin) are about 200 times sweeter than table sugar. Saccharin (Sweet 'N Low, Sweet Twin and Necta Sweet) is between 200 and 700 times sweeter than sugar, and sucralose (Splenda) about 600 times sweeter. The new kids on the block, neotame (Newtame) and Advantame, are between 7,000 and 20,000 times sweeter than sugar and have just been approved by the FDA for general use in the United States.

People tend to drink products containing these sweeteners because they are marketed as diet drinks, so they perceive them to be healthy and calorie-free. This then leads to poor dietary choices, which causes weight gain, obesity and a number of other health ills. It has been linked to heart attacks, stroke and Type II diabetes.

The ideal way to 'rehabilitate' your taste buds is to cut out hidden sugar and sweeteners of all varieties. You will find that you become much more sensitive to lower amounts of any sweet substance.

Wealthy Body Wisdom: 95 per cent of all decisions we make are based on previously established habits. However, habits can change if you want them to...

Alcohol

Alcohol is a fascinating chemical. It is a poison that dulls our nervous system. But for some reason, humans find this a wonderful sensation. With consistent increased intake over months and years, it suppresses the immune system, reducing access to the feel-good hormones serotonin and dopamine (the motivational hormone). It also interferes with good digestion, causing the digestive tract to become more permeable (leaky) over time, leading to conditions such as leaky gut, bloating, allergies, fatigue and weight gain.

> **Wealthy Body Wisdom:** *Drinking two glasses of wine will give you the same amount of calories as eating a cheeseburger.*

New research published in the *American Journal of Public Health*[2] reveals what many of us have known for some time: even just a couple of glasses of wine a day can pose a serious long-term threat to your health.

That piece of news may come as a surprise to those of us in business (where drinking is an accepted part of the culture) and those of us who have embraced the popular notion that moderate drinking makes alcohol a healthy substance to drink.

Newsflash: it's not.

Alcohol is by definition a neurotoxin, a diuretic, a depressant, a carcinogen and a testosterone suppressant.

Yet we fool ourselves into buying into the myth that so long as we're not bingeing, drinking less but more frequently is healthy.

There is also a strong belief that a fine wine is better for you than a cheap one.

Wrong again.

Yes, we all like to think we're somehow more refined, educated, aware or appreciative of something that's been crafted and nurtured over the years so it forms a substance perfect in texture, colour, 'nose' or taste.

Yet once it runs over our tongue and olfactory sensors and passes into our guts, the body doesn't know or care any different. All it says to itself is, *Alcohol, shmalcohol: now let's get it the heck out of the system.* You may drink only bottles of wine that cost hundreds – but if you have too much you'll be as sick as a dog, the same as the guy who gets smashed on lager. That should help clue you in that it's all the same.

So, we continue to hear a lot of talk about the health benefits of drinking wine. Red wine in particular. Popular thinking attributes this to an antioxidant called resveratrol, which is found in the skin of dark grapes (which, interestingly enough, is the part of the grape that isn't generally used in winemaking). Now there have been numerous studies that show resveratrol can control, and even reverse, cancer in rats. But we need a reality check here. This is in rats, not humans, and if the benefits did actually transfer to humans, you would have to drink *25 bottles of wine a day* to get the same amount of resveratrol as contained in one capsule you can buy from the health shop.

You also need to know that most wines you buy today contain a toxic mix of chemicals and agrochemical traces that have been attributed to the headache you get the next day – chemicals absent from organic wines.

In addition, alcohol *causes* – not cures – cancer. Way back in 1988 the World Health Organization classed alcohol as one of *the most carcinogenic* [cancer-causing] *substances* in the human diet, and at least 15 per cent of all breast cancers are directly caused by alcohol.[3]

So this belief about 'good alcohol' is completely false – and you continue to accept this notion at your peril.

You see, the question all hinges on the definition of 'healthy'. In our opinion, healthy nutrition is anything which, when consumed, advances or contributes to your health position. So even drinking water can be unhealthy by that definition – if you drink too much.

We've all heard the saying, *everything in moderation*, and to a certain degree that's true. Remember, though, that what the saying refers to is the degree to which we can *get away with it* without our health suffering. That's a very different thing to actually *advancing* your health position. And anyway – would you run your business in this haphazard fashion?

Even imbibing small quantities of alcohol, regardless of its form, will affect your mental acuity, mood, energy levels and therefore your overall health position – and possibly your lifespan. Just ask the relatives of the 40,000 people who die every year in the UK from drinking alcohol.

Next time you have a drink in your hand, look deep into the glass. There is nothing good going on in there.

Now, we're not against drinking alcohol – bet that surprised you. It's probably OK to have a drink or two on a special occasion. But understand this: occasions happen *occasionally*. 'Evening' is not a special occasion – it happens every day.

So if you're adhering to a largely healthy eating and exercise regime, and advancing your health position by ten steps, and every now and again (occasionally) taking a step sideways – well, you're still nine steps ahead.

And in our book that's OK, because you're making alcohol part of a balanced and socially functional lifestyle. (Whether alcohol is something that has a place in business culture – especially if you consider yourself a high performer – is a whole other debate.)

But don't for a minute believe that alcohol is a healthy substance – in any quantity.

It ain't.

The Wealthy Body Food Pyramid

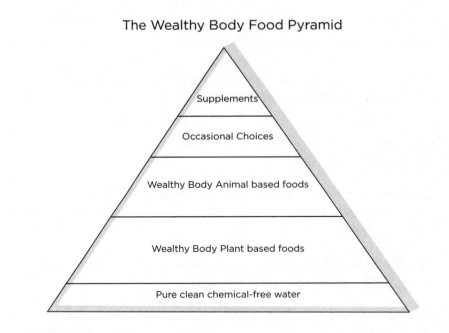

Supplements

Occasional Choices

Wealthy Body Animal based foods

Wealthy Body Plant based foods

Pure clean chemical-free water

Examples:

Wealthy Body plant-based foods: Asparagus, aubergine, avocados, broccoli, Brussels sprouts, cabbage, cauliflower, capsicums, celery, cucumber, runner beans, lettuce, onions, beetroot, mushrooms, olives, raw almonds, onions, spinach, snap peas, kale, chard, tomato, watercress, zucchini, nuts, seeds, sprouts, green powders, herbs, spices, vinegars, unsweetened almond milk, coconut milk, olive Oil, coconut oil, avocado oil, macadamia or nut-based oils and butters.

Wealthy Body animal-based foods: Organic free-range pasture-fed beef, lamb, pork, poultry, game, sustainable wild-caught fish, seafood, butter, cheese, cream, eggs, cottage cheese, organ meats. organic plain yogurt, raw whole milk, goats' milk

Occasional Choices: Pumpkin, sweet potatoes, carrots, peas, yams, parsnip, fruit, organic raw dark chocolate 85-90% cocoa, raw cacao, natural sweeteners (stevia, natvia, xylitol), alcohol

Supplements: Multi-vitamins, multi-minerals, specific vitamins and minerals as prescribed or recommended.

Foods to avoid: Cereal grains and flours (especially processed grains), sweeteners (aspartame, acesulfame), commercially manufactured diet foods, GMO foods, high fructose corn syrup, soy milk and tofu, margarines, pasta, potatoes, sugar, highly processed vegetable and seed oils (canola, sunflower, rice bran, soya, grape seed, corn, sunflower and palm oil), syrups, fruit canned in syrups, flavoured milk, sweetened flavoured yogurts, highly processed / deep fried meats (nuggets etc), energy drinks, fruit juices, fruit-flavoured drinks, soft drinks/soda, artificial sweeteners, high-carb protein bars.

Wealthy Body Action Points

1. To stay sharp and on top of your game, don't drink alcohol during the working week.

2. To relax and be sociable in good company, give yourself permission to have a maximum of two drinks on Friday and two drinks on Saturday.

3. Never drink on an empty stomach. Always have a meal when you have a drink to slow down the absorption of alcohol into your bloodstream.

4. Alternate sips of alcohol with sips of water to reduce the volume and pace of alcohol you're drinking.

5. If someone pours a drink for you, just take a sip, then sit on it for the rest of the evening – no one will notice.

6. Alternatively, keep topping up a champagne glass with sparkling water with a dash of apple juice. Everyone will think you're having a great time…!

7. Avoid salty foods around alcohol – they will make you feel thirstier. That's why pubs and bars offer peanuts and other salty snacks. Get it?

Nutritional Myths and Myth-information™

Things we have come to believe that may not actually be true.

The Truth about Eggs

Eggs have had a bad rap in the past, being slammed for containing too much fat and cholesterol – but that's old thinking. They are one of the most nutritious foods on the planet. They are nature's ultimate multi-vitamin, containing an enormous amount of nutrients compared to their calorie load.

In fact in recent studies, subjects who dramatically increased their dietary consumption of eggs showed no corresponding increase in serum (blood) cholesterol levels, and noted beneficial gains in nutrient profiles.[4]

A hard-boiled egg is also a fantastic portable food to take to the office – easy to tuck away in your bag, and they come conveniently packaged in their own carry shell. They are quick to prepare and eat, and they're low in calories with only around 80 calories per medium egg – so they are great if you're on a diet.

Having an egg or two will stop hunger in its tracks, because they're a high-NDF (nutrient-dense food)!

Whole eggs have the perfect essential amino acid profile to sustain your physique. These specific amino acids cannot be produced in your body, so you must get them from the foods you eat.

Eggs are also rich in lutein and zeaxanthin – essential ingredients for eye health – which are difficult to source in other foods.

Another health benefit of eggs is their source of choline, a fat-soluble nutrient that's a key component of many structures in cell membranes. Two fat-like molecules in the brain – phosphatidylcholine and sphingomyelin – account for an unusually high percentage of the brain's total mass, so choline is particularly important for brain function and health.

Organic eggs are also rich in vitamin D, and in omega-3 fats – particularly the long-chain DHA and DPA, representing up to 127 per cent of the adequate daily intake. Omega-3 is found in cell membranes in the brain and the eyes. It has anti-inflammatory properties and plays a major role in infant growth and development, and protection against diseases.

Anything that contains all the ingredients to start a new life has got to be good for you! Notice how all the smartest animals in the wild go for eggs when hunting for the richest nutrient sources.

It's important to keep in mind, however, that not all eggs are created equal. Hens are often raised in factories, caged, and fed on grain- or soy-based feed that alters the final nutrient composition of the eggs. They may also be exposed to growth hormones, antibiotics and other veterinary drugs.

The best eggs to buy are farm-fresh, organic, free-range eggs that have been allowed to roam free to feed on bugs, seeds and grasses – their natural food sources in the wild.

Finally, eggs are cheap, tasty and go with almost any food. The nutrients are found in the yolks, while the whites are mostly protein. In fact, they contain around 10g of protein per egg – about the same as a lean lamb chop!

Wealthy Body Action Points

1. Boil half a dozen eggs ahead of time and place one or two in a sandwich bag, ready to eat for a snack.

2. Travel tip: when having breakfast at the hotel buffet, order an omelette made with minimal oil, and add lots of peppers, mushrooms, tomato and onions. Poached eggs on wholemeal are a good breakfast option too! Ask for a couple of hard-boiled eggs 'to go' – they beat airport food hands down!

3. Boiled eggs go great in salads as a source of protein if you're not eating meat.

I like sweet foods.
Only eat sweet foods as you would find them in nature. They come in their correct parcel of fibre and synergist ingredients without extra added refined sugar and chemicals as in man-made sweet treats. It is less fattening and better for your health to eat your fruit than drink it!

I eat lots of fruit, is this OK for training?
It is better to combine carbohydrate foods with protein to make up a snack. An apple is considered a carbohydrate food. An example of a protein food is cottage cheese. So to make a balanced snack to support your training, you'd eat an apple with a portion of cottage cheese. To make up a more substantial meal, combine more complex carbohydrates (vegetables) with protein (a chicken breast, for example).

I Don't Eat Meat – I Eat Fish Because It's Better

Part of being healthy is knowing where your food comes from, and being educated on how humanely it was reared. Fish and fish supplements are big business and the health food industry has a lot to answer for in the depletion of our fish stocks. Many studies have now sunk the myth that eating fish is good for your health, because after years of using our oceans as a waste dump, fish and fish oil supplements are regularly found to be contaminated with high levels of mercury, polychlorinated biphenyls and other industrial pollutants. With wild species now over-fished and depleted, the industry has turned to farmed fish. But when fish are kept in confined conditions, 'good' turns to 'bad'.

Intensive battery-farmed fish have to be dyed and dosed with pharmaceuticals to keep them the right colour and the right size, and also to survive the parasites and diseases rife in this unnatural environment. Being turned into a couch potato and kept away from its natural free-range environment changes the healthy omega oil profile of fish and lowers the useable protein content. As with humans, pollutants accumulate in the fat cells of fish, which is then distilled into concentrated fish oil supplements for human consumption. Common intensively farmed fish include salmon, caro, tilapia, sea bass, catfish and cod.

Having had these dangers highlighted in the wider media, the industry has now seized upon krill, which are tiny shrimplike crustaceans that are approximately 1–6cm (0.3–2.3 inches) long. They live in the ocean, where they feed mainly on phytoplankton. They're near the bottom of the food chain and don't live long enough to become polluted. They are eaten by whales, seals, penguins, squid and fish – and concerns have now been raised that the popularity among humans of krill oil supplements could threaten the population of these important predators who rely on this food source to survive and flourish.

Our oceans used to be a finely balanced ecosystem. How can we possibly believe that plundering hundreds of thousands of tonnes of fish from these waters every year will not affect this self-governing balance?

We have more good reasons than ever to leave fish in the water where they belong. We all know that the human body is a group of finely balanced and intricate systems. Well, so is our planet. The way we have been consuming fish has an enormous impact on the bottom line of both. Curb your desire to eat fish regularly, as it may have more worrying longer-term health implications than advertising will ever let us believe. When man interferes in nature it usually ends in tears.

Eat fat, polluted food, and you will become fat and polluted.

Aren't All Calories Equal?

This is another myth that doesn't die. The 'calorie myth' is one of the most pervasive – and most damaging – in the health and well-being industry.

I was recently presenting to an executive team in the EU when an older gentleman with pallid grey skin stood up and challenged me on this. I had been talking about the difference to health between calorie energy and vitality energy.

'It's physics,' he insisted. 'If you eat the same calories as you burn, you'll maintain the same weight.' An interesting theory. However, the actual science is overwhelmingly clear on this point.

Suppose you have a 100-calorie banana in one hand and a 100-calorie doughnut in the other. Do you view them as being the same because the number of calories is the same?

This says everything that needs to be said about the limitations of just using calories in guiding our food choices.

One is packed with vitamins and minerals – and the other isn't. One has enzymes – and the other doesn't. One has lots of soluble fibre – and the other doesn't. Oh, and one has lots of trans-fat and sugar – and the other doesn't. One will sustain and nourish you, and the other will suck the life and energy from you.

Different foods go through different biochemical pathways, and it is vital to recognise that different foods and macronutrients have a major effect on the hormones and brain centres that control hunger, mood, energy and eating behaviour. Different types of sugars and sweeteners also distort your biochemistry, and that may actually lead to weight gain.

So all calories are *not* equal in the effect they have on the body, and counting calories will not help you lose weight and become healthier and more energised if you are consuming the *wrong kind* of calories.

In short:

» Calorie calculations don't take into account the nutritional content and properties of the food you're eating, and the effect they have on your body systems and health.
» Calorie values of foods are calculated by completely incinerating a food in a Bomb Calorimeter. This is *not* how your body works biologically, as not everything you eat is burned as fuel.
» There are no valid studies to support the 'calories in – calories out' theory. Yes, this references a law of physics, but it doesn't apply completely here – the calculative assumption is wrong. And besides, there are just far too many other variables.
» Even if the model was relevant, calories and weight should not be your focus when thinking about nutrition. More important is body composition, tone, shape, health, energy, well-being, vitality and mental acuity.

Our message is this: you don't have to be a doctor, rocket scientist or a media personality to be energetic, sexy and strong. You just have to have an open mind, consider all the current information carefully, and consider that if it doesn't make sense, it probably isn't true.

I Don't Have Time to Count Calories

Great! Those who have lost weight and kept it off, and those with the greatest success in maintaining good shape as they age, literally have no idea how many calories they're eating each day. People who work with us have to become knowledgeable and aware of nutrient-dense foods (NDFs) – and at that point, calorie counts are of very little concern.

If I Eat Less, I'll Lose Weight Healthily

Why do we suggest you eat 4–5 small meals a day?

Several studies have focused on employee productivity and the attention patterns of children in relation to their morning eating habits.

They've concluded that the benefits, in terms of energy and mental focus, of a low-GL (glycaemic load, which refers to the sugar absorption rate of an entire meal, as opposed to GI, which measures just a single ingredient) *high-protein* breakfast aren't only felt in the morning, but extend through the day as well.[5]

The average adult turns over 300g (10oz) of protein a day. Eighty per cent of that is recycled, broken down and re-used, a bit like Lego bricks, but after a certain period of time these proteins become worn out and are lost to the body.

What we cannot salvage, we need to replace, and once you start skipping meals you will compromise your ability to take in enough. For the serious trainer (that's you), this is physique suicide as the body starts breaking down muscle.

Normally active men and women require a minimum of 1.5g protein per kilo of lean bodyweight – just over 0.7g per pound. (Lean bodyweight is your total weight on the scales, less the amount of your weight that's fat. So if you weigh 60kg (132lb), with 25 per cent body fat (that's 15kg/33lb), your lean weight is 45kg (99lb). Multiply that by 1.5 and your protein intake per day should be more than 67.5g. For those actively exercising or training, the requirement goes up to a minimum of 2g per kilo of lean bodyweight.

The main problem is that your body can only effectively absorb and utilise 20–30g of protein at one sitting. So, to get enough protein into your day, it will need to be spread out over at least four meals.

Protein is non-negotiable – even your bones are 50 per cent protein – and unlike other essential micronutrients, you need it every single day. The ordinary sedentary male may have a higher reserve of muscle they can call on for protein during the fasting days. But this approach is dangerous if you are working out hard. (Is there any other way?)

Human studies have been limited on this type of dieting and so far they have all lacked control groups and have used short trial lengths. A handful of smaller, well-controlled studies on fasting reveal that women may actually miss out on the much-touted improvements in glucose tolerance and insulin responses because of their lower muscle mass, and this could increase their risk of developing osteoporosis, diabetes, hormone imbalances and weight gain as they age.

I am always afraid that I will gain weight on any plan where I have to eat regularly. It's difficult for me to find time to eat at work.
It's difficult for a lot of people to 'find time' to get all of their daily nutrients in – that's why taking your own food to the office, or when you're out and about, is vital. In emergencies, or if you get really stuck, meal or protein shakes also offer a fast, convenient top-up. Ask anybody in fantastic shape what their secret is and they will tell you it is being organised and disciplined with their food arrangements. In our experience no-one ever got into great shape by missing meals (or eating out, come to that).

How will I know if this is working?
Keep a log book of changes and measurements. You need to know what is working and what isn't working. Don't become one of those many people who do exactly the same thing for months and months and never seem to see any change.

When we are told to drink plenty of water a day, how big a glass or how many ounces per day?
Six tall glasses a day is a good rule of thumb. There's not a universal requirement. People who exercise regularly need even more. We drink water, herbal teas and sip on half a lemon or grapefruit blended with water (for a little flavour) during the day, so probably the equivalent of eight glasses of water in total.

Is sparkling water OK to drink? Can it count towards my daily water intake?
Yes, it's a good substitute for alcohol when dining out, and the bubbles have a festive feel! Be aware, though, that because the CO_2 in sparkling water is acidic, you may be wise to reserve this strategy for special occasions.

I don't like eating whole wheat or brown rice. Can we just stick to regular white rice and bread?

No. Remember the saying, 'The whiter the bread, the sooner you're dead'! These foods are missing all the healthy nutrients vital for your health. People who regularly eat heavily processed foods such as these get disease early. You will also notice they have a gluten pallor to their skin. White rice can increase your insulin levels by as much as 20 per cent, whereas brown rice will decrease insulin levels by 10 per cent. If you care for your spouse tell them to harden up and not behave like such a child around food!

How do I control my portion sizes? I have been raised to eat hearty!
Each person's portion sizes will be different. Remember, a portion of protein for you is about the size of the palm of your hand. A portion of carbohydrate is an amount roughly equal to the size of your clenched fist. And a whole meal should fit into the area of both your hands cupped together. Tip: downsize your dinner plate, think airline-sized servings, and remember that the more nutrient-dense foods you eat, the less you have to scoff.

Even if I eat a balanced meal, I always seem to be hungry within a few hours. I could eat all day.
You can eat every 2–3 hours throughout the day as long as it is high-vitality food, isn't off a large plate and isn't processed junk. Eating little and often (the key word here is 'little') throughout the day supports your energy and muscle metabolism, while helping you burn body fat. We are intrigued by vastly obese people who say they can't stop eating, and that they are addicted to food; when you look closely, what they are addicted to is rubbish. If you put a banquet of fresh steamed vegetables in front of them, they would be cured of their eating addiction in about 5 minutes.

I'm very busy in my role. How can I keep on top of the nutrition side of things?
For time-pressed executives, the trick lies in making healthy eating both realistic and strategic. Being healthy doesn't mean avoiding all your favourite foods – it's simply about managing your menus, and your schedule!

Here are our Seven Commandments:

1. Do eat breakfast
2. Have healthy snacks to hand – don't fall into the trap of dipping into the muffin display during a meeting
3. Get a handle on work colleague/client drinking
4. Always go for nutrient-dense foods (NDFs)
5. Substitute processed grains and sugars with more healthy fats
6. Plan your meals like you plan your meetings
7. Be wise about size – get tough on portion control

5.
DINING OUT

Eating at restaurants is a social pleasure and a positive life experience. But because we, as customers, have little control over the quality of the food being served, it can be easy to write the whole experience off as an indulgence. Your Wealthy Body need not deny itself the experience of a night out, especially when you can still exert some influence over your intake.

» Find a restaurant you can return to again and again – the staff will get to know you, and your ordering preferences. This makes getting the meal you want easier each time.

» Eat something healthy before you go out. By the time you are seated at the restaurant, you'll be ready to order a smaller-portioned meal without over-eating. (This also saves money.)

» As soon as you are seated, drink a full glass of water, and say *no* to the bread basket.

» When ordering, ask to have the preparation of the dishes explained. Which dishes are baked, grilled or fried, and what type of sauces or dressings are they served with?

» Enquire if the vegetables can be steamed, blanched or raw.

» To avoid starchy carbs (potato, pasta, rice), ask if you can load up on the 'greens' instead.

» Never hesitate to ask for food to be prepared exactly the way you want it. We are continually amazed at the number of very senior people in business who don't seem to have the backbone to ask for their food to be prepared the way they need it to be. Who is paying whom here? Would you run your division like that? You end up with what you tolerate, and everyone will see it on your hips.

» Often restaurants serve helpings that are at least twice the normal size. Don't feel bad about asking for a half-portion.

» If you are treating yourself to a dessert or sweet, investigate and order the items lowest in cheap fats, stodgy carbs and sugar.

» If you will be dining at a new restaurant, make the reservation yourself so you can advise the staff well ahead of your preferences, or task your assistant with this responsibility. This also allows you to check if the restaurant can assist with your food choices or not. It may be that you'll have to choose another venue.

» Never accept second-rate options. Ageing well isn't for sissies – always keep a razor-sharp focus on building a lean, strong physique, a healthy constitution, and a bright and vital presence.

If you feel confident:

» Don't open the menu. Instead order whole-food, nutrient-dense items that you know will be found on any menu, or which can be easily prepared in any kitchen.

» Skip the appetisers and go straight for a consommé soup (one prepared with a water base and natural stock. Avoid anything called 'Cream of...' or 'Crème de...').

» Ask for a main of steamed/grilled/poached fish or meat with steamed vegetables.

» Request that any dressing or sauces be served 'on the side'.

» Go spicy! The temptation to over-eat can be a subconscious response to plain food! Add chillies, peppers, cayenne, curcumin, turmeric, onions or garlic to meats, salads, yogurt dips and scrambled eggs, or curry powder to sauces. Try spicy dishes from the menu, but be sure to check the contents.

Restaurant Spot Checks

Use these as rough guides for the appropriate size of portion to eat when dining out:

» Chicken: palm of the hand
» Fish: palm of the hand
» Salmon and tuna: ½ palm of hand
» Lean beef and pork: ½ palm of hand
» Starchy foods – such as sweet potato, beetroot, yams, pumpkin, etc: 1 teacup
» Fruit: size of a tennis ball

- » Vegetables (greens): 2–3 teacups
- » Oils, dressings: 1 fingertip
- » Organic yogurt: 1 teacup

Drinks to Order

- » Filtered water on ice (with a twist of lemon)
- » Sparkling water
- » Iced or hot herbal teas
- » Dry red or white wine: a maximum of 2 x 150ml (5oz) glasses in any one sitting.
- » Fresh-ground organic coffee occasionally (but not at night, clearly...)
- » Green juice or smoothie

Avoid These Drinks

- » Beer and 'energy' mixers
- » Spirits with soft-drink mixers
- » Soy milk and flavoured soy drinks
- » Soft drinks
- » Diet soft drinks
- » Flavoured milk shakes
- » Juice drinks (usually containing added sugar and other ingredients)
- » Creamy cocktails

Fish and Seafood

Generally seafood is low in damaging fats, high in good fats and high in protein. Much of the damage is done in the preparation and cooking.

- » Avoid all deep-fried fish. Ask for steamed, poached, baked or grilled portions.
- » Specify no added salt or added MSG.
- » Fresh lemon or a twist or two of black pepper is all that is needed for seasoning.

» Choose only fish species from ethically sustainable stocks (www.goodfishguide.org)

Soups

Quiz your server about the exact ingredients and preparation methods for the soup selection. Once you have established this, it makes it very easy to order on future occasions.

» Many vegetable soups have table salt, cheap oils and refined flour added to create extra texture, taste and thickness. Avoid these ingredients if possible.

Asking these sorts of questions will assist in determining the standard of preparation, degree of healthy ingredients and levels of nutrients in your soup choices.

If you are at home, remember the following points:

» The best vegetable soup is simply puréed vegetables with only seasoning added. Simmering a little water off the stock, or adding potato or rice can add thickness.
» At home, unsweetened Greek yogurt can be used as a topping instead of cream or sour cream. It may also be used to give a creamy texture to lobster bisque.
» Instead of sautéeing vegetables in oil for a minestrone, sweat them in a light stock on a high heat.

Sandwich Secrets

Avoid sandwich bread wherever possible. With modern mass-batch refining and processing, most of the nutritious elements found in the whole grains that bread is supposed to be made from are missing. It simply isn't made like it used to be.

Out for lunch? Alternatively, you can order your sandwiches with double greens: the thickness of the greens should be at least as high as the bottom bread and meat! You can also order an 'open' sandwich by losing the top slice of bread. Better yet, ditch the sandwich altogether and get a salad bowl with grilled fish – like tuna, salmon or shrimp – or chicken.

Vital Vegetables: The Secret to Longevity

You're always a winner when you choose vegetables to accompany a meal. They are truly nutrient-dense foods (NDFs). Eat as many high-colour, crunchy, fibrous veggies as possible to load up on nutrition, and you can have them grilled, steamed, baked, blended (as in a smoothie) or raw. Use vegetables or organic bones as the base of any soup stock. Remember it's not the vegetables themselves that make you fat, but the method with which they are prepared.

» For a midday meal, don't be afraid of eating starchy vegetables or grains (sweet potatoes, pumpkin, quinoa and wild rice) with your fibrous mixture – you'll need the extra energy to get through the afternoon.
» For afternoon and evening meals, choose mixed high-coloured vegetables instead – spinach, broccoli, Brussels sprouts, peppers (capsicums), asparagus, pak-choi, salad greens, grated beetroots, etc.

Salads

Organic salads are grown healthy but are then destroyed in the kitchen. Avoid any dressings containing cheap mayonnaise or oils. While there is an abundance of dressings available in the supermarkets, it is not beyond the wit and drive of most chefs to prepare a similar recipe if a herbal tang is required. If need be, simply ask for a drizzle of good-quality balsamic vinegar, Greek yogurt or perhaps chilli sauce.

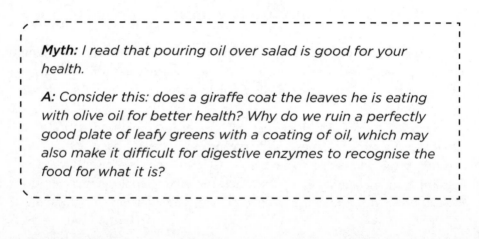

Myth: I read that pouring oil over salad is good for your health.

A: Consider this: does a giraffe coat the leaves he is eating with olive oil for better health? Why do we ruin a perfectly good plate of leafy greens with a coating of oil, which may also make it difficult for digestive enzymes to recognise the food for what it is?

Here's our view on this: Whole food is the key, as it comes with its own package of synergistic nutrients and essential fibre. Isolated fats are just that: processed and isolated. Just like we understand that isolated sugars are not a good thing, we will need to understand that isolated fats are not a good thing either. Eat the olive not the commercial olive oil; eat the orange, not the commercial juice!

Poultry

Chicken, turkey, quail and even ostrich are all of the same biological structure, so what is true of chicken is true for all poultry. Always choose free-range organic meats; they will be free from chemical residues like pesticides, insecticides, herbicides, fungicides, growth hormones, veterinary antibiotics and other man-made chemicals. Remember: we eat what our food eats! The animals will also be leaner, contain correct ratios of omega-3 fats, and have lived happier, healthier lives.

» White meat (breast) is leanest, and dark meat has a higher fat content (thighs, wings). Don't be afraid, just aware.
» Avoid crispy skin on chicken, pan-frying, fricasséeing, or any preparation method that involves superheated fats or oils.

Red Meats – Beef, Lamb and Pork

» Check for country of origin. New Zealand beef and lamb is a good choice, as it's mostly free-range and pasture-fed.
» When ordering, be aware that leanest choices are tenderloin, top sirloin and topside. Fattest steak cuts are porterhouse, rib, rib-eye, T-bone, brisket and chuck steak.
» A single serving of steak should be about the same size as the palm of your hand (about 175g/6oz).
» Choose lamb leg steaks or loin as the least fatty portions.
» Select free-range and organic pork wherever possible.
» Avoid streaky bacon, processed ham and crackling.

» Eat more than just 'muscle' meats – bone stock and organ meats seem to have fallen out of favour lately, but they are traditionally rich sources of a wider variety of nutrients. In nature, the smartest predators always consume the organs of their prey first. Don't say 'Eeew', open your mind and change your irrational beliefs.

» Avoid high-fat cuts such as salami, pastrami, bologna or burgers.

» Sausages, frankfurters and savaloys tend to be predominantly made from fatty off-cuts and breadcrumbs, likewise with recipes containing sausage meat. Savouries, pasties, samosas and sausage rolls have fat-rich pastry, as well as containing very little in the way of protein or other nutrition.

Desserts

Common sense is your main guide here – fresh fruit salads are best, though quite sweet, and you'll know to minimise the size of the serving if you decide to treat yourself to richer fare.

If you need that slice of cake, share it with someone. Cut it in half, or even quarters.

If you can stick to two – OK, three – forkfuls of cake, you will yield the same pleasure as having eaten an entire slice, without the long-term repercussions.

Wealthy Body Wisdom: The esoteric pleasure of chocolate and other dessert flavours comes from the first two bites. After this, taste receptors become overloaded. Every subsequent bite has less pleasure than the one before it.

***Wealthy Body Action Points:** When dining out, whether with family, a client or colleagues, check the menu options online to ensure you can get the right choices, before you book the restaurant.*

If you're a guest at someone else's dinner function, phone the chef the day before to see if they have the options you'd prefer. It saves any fuss or embarrassment on the night with the waiting staff.

If in doubt, eat a small nutritious meal before you leave home. By pre-empting hunger, this will prevent you eating too much later in the evening, and you can choose to leave less healthy items to the side of your plate.

6.
YOUR BRAIN

Keeping Your Intelligence in Peak Condition

In 2008 researchers discovered that regular physical exercise increased the development of neurons in mice[6], and reversed some of the effects of ageing, including cognitive dysfunction.

So: exercise offers a wide variety of positive effects on the body and brain.

It also has anti-depressant effects. Lab tests found that exercise enhances spatial learning in both young and aged mice and increases plasticity in the hippocampus, a key structure for cognitive function and stress-related pathologies such as depression.[7] In addition, research conducted by Professor Maria Fiatarone Singh[8], showed that heavy weight-lifting reduced depression by as much as 70 per cent in 70-year-olds, and was equally effective in managing the condition as the default medication!

This means that your trip to the gym is making you smarter – and happier!

Concentration

There is a myth that our busy lifestyles require substances such as caffeine and sweet snacks, mid-morning and mid-afternoon, to survive lapses of concentration or fatigue. Nowhere, it seems, do we feel that need more than in the workplace.

A primary reason for this is that none of us really wants to be there. Yes, we want to be successful, but for a lot of people, the workplace presents challenges: deadlines, meetings, co-workers and bosses that we would really rather not have to deal with. Put it this way: if you won really big money in the lottery this weekend, would you be back at the office on Monday? Probably not.

When you are doing something you really like, endorphins take over, and the tasks become easy. The less enjoyable the work, the more oppressive your internal emotional atmosphere becomes, and along with that comes metabolic suppression and depression.

Hence the need for a pick-me-up.

Ironically, it is this type of diet – the one that includes the extra coffee and the sweet snack – that makes us less efficient and can actually hinder our rise to the top. It can even knock us off our perch prematurely.

Recent research from the International Labour Office in Geneva[9] showed that simple things, such as skipping meals or eating nutrient-poor snacks and caffeine, trigger low blood sugar levels, which will shorten attention span and actually *slow* the speed with which you process information.

As reported in *The Times*, the high-flyers of the boardroom such as Sir Richard Branson, Sir Stuart Rose and Dame Amelia Fawcett have one thing in common, and that is a trim waistline, a healthy glow and a commitment to exercise. It's not just about looking good; it's about keeping the brain fit for business well into the high numbers of age.

Now you might say that someone like Richard Branson has all the money in the world, and can therefore afford time for exercise. But along with all that money comes a huge pile of responsibilities and priorities. He has several enormous companies to run, any one of which could easily swallow his entire day. Now if he can make time for exercise, with a to-do list literally the size of a jumbo jet, then so can *You*!

Wealthy Body Action Points

1. Enter your workouts in your diary just as you book your meetings and appointments. A 30-minute session in the gym will be enough to build strength, fitness, shape – and burn fat.

2. The best time to work out is first thing in the morning, when your growth hormone levels are at their peak. Having said that, any time of day is better than none, right?

3. Build before you burn. For the most time-efficient workout, always do your weights before doing any cardio.

4. If it's hard to get time away from the office for training, keep a set of adjustable dumbbells by your desk. Whenever you get 60 seconds between calls or meetings, blast through a quick set of press-ups, dumbbell curls or squats.

5. You can do the same at home too!

6. Keep your legs in great shape by always climbing stairs two at a time. You can do this at any time of the day – even when travelling!

7. Get yourself a standing desk. The act of sitting does more damage to your body than simply not being active. Prolonged sitting shuts down nerve activity in the legs, reduces your calorie-burning ability to little more than lying down, and shunts your fat-burning ability into dormancy. You'll stay more energised, alert, burn more calories and improve your posture – all at the same time!

The Deterioration of Concentration

Concentration is the ability to sustain focused attention on a given subject or object. In fact, you are concentrating right now, as you read these words:

Can you make it right to the end? Can your ability to concentrate empower you to identify the problem with this triangular sign?

Concentration can be external – such as relating to other people or driving – or it can be internal – such as thoughts, feelings or sensations.

The power of concentration also involves the ability to pay no attention to irrelevant distractions. Like concentration itself, these intrusions can be divided into external and internal distractions.

External distractions relate to the physical environment – noise, interruptions from other people, televisions, work responsibilities, and so on. Internal distractions relate to your body, your thoughts and emotions, such as hunger, tiredness, illness, pain, boredom and stress.

Some of these can be easily dealt with once they are identified. The reasons behind continuing poor concentration – that is, when it feels like a permanent, irreversible condition – are either related to some form of brain impairment (whether due to accident or disease) or to age-related deterioration that can take place in the brain, depending on your state of health.

Age-Related Mental Decline

Aside from the various forms of age-related dementia, it is likely that up to a third of adults will experience a gradual decline in their mental capabilities as they get older. Symptoms of mental deterioration, such as short-term memory loss and difficulties in learning new information, may not interfere with everyday life, but they are sufficient to impair concentration and memory.

This decline is due to many factors that accumulate over the years, contributing to damaging changes in our brains as we get older. Clinical tests demonstrate that diets with high sugar/trans-fat intake produce significantly higher risks of mental deterioration, especially in the hippocampus.[10]

Similarly stress studies have shown that stress – both everyday stress and major traumatic stress – causes a rise in the stress hormone epinephrine, which can lead to mild cognitive impairment. In many cases our responses to stress are directly influenced by the quality of our diet and the exercise we get.

Wealthy Body Wisdom: The difference between being mentally sharp and senility is, in terms of brain neuron firing speed, only a matter of a few milliseconds...

Myth: My grandfather has Alzheimer's therefore I will get it.

A: No, not necessarily. This decline in cognitive ability is due to many factors that accumulate over the years, contributing to damaging changes in our brains as we get older. For example, men with big bellies are more susceptible to dementia, people with high homocysteine levels lose brain mass, and those who exercise vigorously as they age actually improve their neural capacity. (Please see page 102 for further information on homocysteine.)

Vascular Disease

Cerebrovascular disease occurs in the arteries that pass blood to the brain. The result is a reduced rate of blood flow, which in turn causes nerve cells in the brain to die prematurely. This was demonstrated in a study of 400 middle- to old-aged men, which revealed that vascular risk factors, such as excessive alcohol intake and higher than normal homocysteine levels, are associated with reduced mental processing capacity and information processing speed.[11]

Wealthy Body Action Points

1. To keep your arteries clear and increase blood supply to the brain, make sure you stay as active as possible during the day.

2. Drink around six glasses of pure water throughout the day to maintain low blood viscosity.

3. Cut your coffee and alcohol consumption by at least half from right now.

Free Radicals

These are unstable molecules that are prone to react with other molecules in a damaging process known as oxidation. Areas of the body with high energy output, such as the brain, are particularly vulnerable to damage from free radicals. Animal studies have suggested that diets high in antioxidants and dietary nutrients can delay age-related memory loss.[12]

Wealthy Body Action Point: Supplement with a high-quality multi-vitamin and mineral to protect and support your immune system.

Inflammation

A number of studies have found a clear link between inflammation and cognitive impairment.[13] Symptoms including high blood pressure, high insulin levels, central obesity and abnormal blood lipid levels, as well as high inflammation markers, were more likely to lead to cognitive impairment.

All of these negative health issues bring about changes to the brain that are associated with a reduction of mental capacity. A crucial consequence is the decrease in the number of neurotransmitters in the brain, such as serotonin and acetylcholine – two of the crucial on/off switches for our nervous system.

In addition, the number of nerve impulses and nerve cells will also reduce, and the quantity of blood passing through the brain will diminish. This is particularly important as the oxygen and nutrients that are required for the brain to function correctly are carried into the brain by the blood.

Fortunately, many of the problems associated with executive memory loss and other neurological disturbances are correctable. Too often in the past, physicians have viewed these detrimental changes to the brain as an inevitable consequence of ageing. Indeed, conventional medicine has had little to offer people who visit their physician describing a small decline in their memory or mental abilities.

Recent developments, however, have uncovered a number of possible causes behind 'age-related' mental decline and identified therapies to enable people to confront and remedy it.

Wealthy Body Action Point: If you have a big belly, measure your waist circumference and weight once a week. Aim to reduce both by at least a small amount each time you measure.

What Can Be Done About It?

Once again, the best way to maintain a healthy, active brain and a sharp intellect is to maintain a healthy, active body. This means:

» plenty of exercise (both weight-bearing and aerobic – in that order)
» a balanced diet (a minimum of 6–9 coloured vegetables per day, along with raw fruit, lean organic protein and increase healthy fats for the brain)
» a good night's sleep
» getting your hormones checked and balanced
» living in an unpolluted environment

If you are not receiving sufficient nourishment, whether through illness, neglect or poor eating habits, your mental capacity will drop dramatically. By stepping up your nutrition by even just a little, you can supercharge your intellect and protect your mind, your body and your business into old age.

Wealthy Body Action Point: Aim to get to bed around 10.30 p.m. every night. Sleep research shows your brain cells regenerate better by getting to bed earlier.

Quality sleep is the missing link to mental performance and physical health. Sleep deprivation affects the hippocampus of the brain – the part of your brain that operates memory. The result? Sleep-deprived people fail to recall pleasant memories, but they remember gloomy memories very well. Sleep loss also debilitates the body's ability to extract glucose from the blood, increasing the hormone ghrelin, which signals hunger, and reducing leptin, which suppresses appetite. It also stimulates the stress hormone cortisol, which has other debilitating effects on your body. Human growth hormone is also disrupted – normally secreted as a single big pulse at the beginning of sleep, it is essential for repair and maintenance.

To get an earlier night's sleep, try bringing your bedtime back by 15 minutes a night so that the change is a gradual one.

Another tip is do not drink alcohol during the working week. This is a strategic decision based on science. When you sleep, particularly in the REM (rapid eye movement) phase, a process takes place where your short-term memory is converted to long-term memory. In other words, the things that you've learned that day are embedded into your memory for recall later on. This is a process called long-term potentiation (or LTP). There is one key thing that interferes or switches off the LTP process, which is alcohol. The next day, this can lead to a failure to retain key facts, figures or statistics that you might need in your high-pressure role. It can lead to slow and sluggish thinking and foggy-headedness, and those are key things you need to overcome in order to remain on top of the game.

Smartness

In the world of high-stakes poker, an inscrutable poker face is essential. A gambling tournament can go on for hours with hundreds of thousands, even millions riding on the outcome. A winning player needs to be at the top of his or her game.

Annie Duke, one of the best poker players in the world, stays at that lofty position by remaining in the best physical shape possible. She says being in optimal physical condition is vital to her concentration and mental stamina during these long events. She performs an intense mixture of weight and cardio training and eats a clean diet.

Nishant Kasibhatla, known as the Grand Master of Memory, can memorise the sequence of a deck of shuffled cards in less than two minutes and can resolve the Rubik's Cube in 90 seconds. He holds records for memorising a 1,944-digit number and a 705-digit binary code. He also holds a Guinness world record for his forwards and backwards recall of a 400-digit binary number. He attributes this amazing brainwork to eating well and to keeping physically fit.

Eight times World Memory Champion Dominic O'Brien, who successfully recalled 54 shuffled decks of cards after seeing each one once, stops drinking alcohol and trains daily for eight months before the competition.

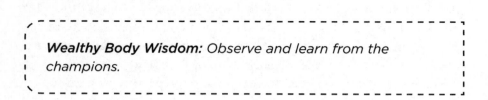

> All the best negotiators negotiate at the end of the day. Why? Because they know they will get the best deal while the other party's guard is down. Eat small, highly nutritious meals throughout the day, and don't rely on snack food.

Wealthy Body Wisdom: Observe and learn from the champions.

7.
YOUR GUT: YOUR SECOND BRAIN

If there is one thing that is definitely emerging in modern-day understanding of psychological health, it is the link between our thoughts, feelings and physical sensations and our body's biochemistry.

What we think changes how we feel. How we feel affects what we eat. This, in turn, affects how we feel!

Never forget that some foods can make you tired. Once eaten, they can make you feel fatigued, affect your mood, disrupt concentration, increase anxiety and stimulate hyperactivity. They can even sap your motivation. Additionally, when you *don't* eat the right foods, the resulting deficiencies in essential vitamins and minerals have been implicated in chronic fatigue, neural dysfunction, obesity and depression.

Conventional psychiatric diagnoses are based on psychological symptoms, and the treatments are based on counselling and giving drugs. The missing link in this approach is the natural biochemical side of this equation, where making lifestyle changes can dramatically improve the way to feeling good while avoiding the use of chemicals, drugs and their very real side effects.

When you feel exhausted, depressed, stressed or anxious, the chances are you won't consider that your digestive system, or the food you've eaten, might have something to do with it.

Our gut and our emotions are linked. Many experts consider our digestive system to be the second brain, since it connects directly with the brain. Just as nervousness or strong emotional feelings can upset your stomach, so foods that don't 'agree with' us can upset our mind.

Witness how, when our mind perceives fear or nervousness, we feel nauseous or get 'butterflies' in the stomach.

Our brain, heart and stomach are connected directly by the vagus nerve – an exclusive self-contained neural loop system. (So what goes in Vagus, stays in Vagus...) Eighty per cent of traffic along this neural pathway travels from the gut to the brain – an important biofeedback mechanism.

More important information about the function and value of this nerve can be found on page 117.

Let's Have a Look at Your Entrails, Shall We?

From front door to back, your digestive tract is about 8m (25–30ft) long. During your lifetime it will process, absorb and eliminate around 80,000lb of food, or 36.5 tonnes – about the same as three and a half London double-decker buses.

The gut lining itself is huge. It makes up a surface area about the size of a tennis court and has half the thickness of a sheet of paper. This is the frontier between you and your food, and it is programmed to react against anything eaten, just in case it is not in your best interest.

It is extremely fragile and easily damaged by too many sugars, grains and processed foods in our diets, which can result in leaky-gut syndrome, irritable bowel syndrome and the formation of thick mucoid plaque.

Every piece of food that you eat has a bearing on how you look and how you feel.

Think about that when you next look at a menu.

There are many factors that contribute to feeling naturally happy and in control, but we shouldn't under-estimate the very basis of feeling good and that is the value of the food choices you make.

Wealthy Body Wisdom: Stop treating your body like a child's new Christmas toy – 'on' today and 'off' tomorrow. Strive for consistency rather than perfection.

8.
YOUR BODY

Energy

Remember when you had tons of energy and sprang out of bed every morning? Me neither.

Seriously, this is not something to be taken for granted, or accepted if it starts to decline. As we age (faster or slower depending on lifestyle habits), our mitochondria (energy cells) also age.

The mitochondria are the powerhouses of our cellular existence. They produce a substance called adenosine triphosphate (ATP), which fuels the body.

In order to manufacture ATP, your body actually has to use existing ATP, which means supplies can be quickly and easily depleted, particularly if you are not feeding it properly, or if you are trying to regain lost energy through caffeine, alcohol or sugar.

'I Used to Get a Slump...'

Not so long ago I ran a well-being seminar for company executives at the Institute of Directors, in London.

During the seminar, one particular man in the audience kept challenging all my main points. He was a well-dressed chap – in his early forties, I guessed; American, judging by the accent; broad across the shoulder but equally as thick around the waist. I answered his questions as best I could and, at the end of the session, he got up and left. I must confess that, in my mind, I wrote him off as a lost cause – one of those inevitable people you get in any audience, and who you're never going to change.

However, not five minutes had passed when my phone rang, and a voice said, 'My name is Phillip. I've just been in your seminar and was wondering if I could sign up to your programme.'

There was much to do, but I enjoy taking on a challenge as much as the next guy. (I say that, as I know he will be reading this.)

In the course of his 24-week programme, we worked together on his exercise regime, optimising sleep patterns, learning the science behind the human physiology and, of course, reinventing his entire nutritional profile. I've seldom worked with a more dedicated and enthusiastic client. In fact, in six months he never missed a single workout!

When we completed his final measurement and photo session (yes, we use photographs as a vital benchmarking and assessment tool), he had lost an incredible amount of weight (38kg/83lb), restored his strength and muscle condition, and massively improved his medical biomarkers.

But more important than this was the difference he told me it made in real terms:

> » Much better sleep, feeling energised and brain up and running in the mornings.
> » Used to get energy slump in the afternoons – doesn't get that now.
> » Thought that taking time out in the middle of the day to work out was a big sacrifice – not the case, as now so much more productive.
> » Now able to achieve more in less time, and others find it hard to keep up..!

There's really nothing more I can add to that.

Here are the most important strategies to keep key earners on top of their game:

> » Get at least 6–8 hours' sleep. This gives your lymphatic system a chance to cleanse itself, your immune system a chance to rebuild itself, and your depleted cells a chance to replenish themselves. By denying your biological 'night cleaning crew' the necessary time to do their job, you open the door to accelerated ageing.
> » Consume the correct fuel. Your cells treat each meal as if it was the last one for a long time (another throwback to the ancient design) and therefore it spends a lot of energy extracting as much nutrition as it can. This means a lot of time and effort can be wasted trying to extract nutrients and energy out of junk foods.

» Cut out the stimulants (caffeine, nicotine, sugar). These provide the opposite of what is sought, and they damage the immune system along the way.

» For a natural energy boost, you can supplement with Coenzyme Q10 (CoQ10) and carnitine, twice a day with breakfast and lunch. CoQ10 is found in every cell. It plays a role in the production of energy and works as an antioxidant to protect the body from otherwise damaging free radicals. Carnitine is an amino acid that transports fatty acids into the mitochondria to be converted into energy.

You don't hear much about magnesium, yet an estimated 80 per cent of us are deficient in this important mineral. The health consequences of magnesium deficiency are significant[14], and symptoms and conditions include insomnia, restlessness, low energy, asthma, blood clots, depression, cramps and diabetes. Researchers have now detected 3,751 magnesium-binding sites on human proteins, indicating that its role in human health and disease may have been vastly under-estimated.[15] Magnesium is also found in more than 300 different enzymes in your body, and is part of the chemical reactions that produce energy, affect digestion and regulate hormones, among other things. It is naturally sourced from organic nuts and seeds, but the *next* best formula is to supplement with magnesium in combination with zinc daily. Magnesium may also be massaged directly into the skin as oil, which is an extremely effective method of delivery.

> **Wealthy Body Wisdom:** *Without health, wisdom cannot reveal itself, art cannot manifest itself, wealth becomes meaningless and intelligence cannot be employed. – Herophilos, 300 BC*

Menopause

'When I asked for a smoking hot body, menopause wasn't what I had in mind!'

We've heard all the jokes, yet as contrived and passé as they are, sadly they are often based in truth. The female body is often analogised as an orchestra – a collection of diverse parts and chemistry that must be coordinated and balanced by hormones that act like the conductor. A successful balance keeps us stable and helps us stay focused on the road ahead.

When we enter the age range between mid-thirties and mid-fifties, the amazing orchestral balance that once made beautiful music in our bodies starts to fluctuate. It struggles with the responsibility of playing both in time and in tune.

First comes peri-menopause. It is an ill-defined phase that occurs before full-blown menopause, when menstruation finally ceases. At this stage, ovarian hormone production declines and fluctuates, which causes a host of somewhat vague yet vexing symptoms. We rarely pay attention to these because they are not specific enough to point to an obvious cause. Many women, and those they turn to – including their doctors – discount the symptoms, not believing them to be menopausal. The typical response is, 'You are not old enough for that.' The symptoms are therefore attributed to stress or to working too hard.

When our hormonal orchestra goes out of tune, a host of unpleasant responses occur. These include a gradual loss of joy, and severe emotional variations: feeling blue one minute, agitated and irritable the next. As menstruation ceases, fatigue, migraines, brain fog, night sweats and hot flushes can dominate and rule the lives of many women. We wake up tired and go to bed 'wired'. We wonder, 'What on earth is happening to me?'

'Is this it for me for the rest of my life?' we ask anybody who will listen. Often, though, it becomes increasingly difficult to feel that anyone is taking these symptoms seriously. As these symptoms start to dominate, successful businesswomen can lose their confidence and their health. They get side-lined with pain-killers, anti-depressants or sleeping tablets.

Mia Lundin, author of *Female Brain Gone Insane*, observes that hard-charging careers may come under threat if businesswomen have difficulty concentrating, become forgetful, sleep poorly or struggle managing stress. Making decisions can become overwhelming and confusing – the consequences can be very severe unless this process of change is managed more effectively.

When the hormones oestrogen, progesterone and testosterone are doing their job properly, they work extremely well together. How much or how little of each hormone is made at any one time depends on a complicated feedback system between the hypothalamus and the pituitary gland, both in the brain. The pituitary releases luteinizing hormone (LH) and follicle stimulating hormone (FSH) in the ovaries and the adrenal glands.

When a woman approaches menopause, oestrogen levels can drop approximately 40 per cent, and progesterone levels can drop up to 90 per cent. Oestrogen stimulates tissue growth, but it needs progesterone to help regulate its efforts. It is when oestrogen levels become too high in comparison to progesterone that the problems occur. To make things worse, a decline in testosterone causes weight gain, loss of libido, motivation and drive. This imbalance is further compounded by environmental toxicity, fatigue, stress, and dietary and lifestyle factors.

Achieving a healthy hormonal balance is a very complicated undertaking since there are many, many players in the orchestra at any given time. When they are correctly balanced, the body can do miraculous things: regenerate new tissue, create an abundance of energy, and defend itself against disease.

Our message is this: don't suffer needlessly through these changes. Get tested, get treated and get better!

Peri-menopause is a perfect time to begin judicious hormone therapy to replace a failing internal supply. Many hormone experts are now concluding that hormone replacement is perfectly safe. It is essential to seek out a qualified specialist practitioner, and only use bio-identical hormones.

It is not acceptable for any woman to be dismissed with an answer such as, 'Your hormones are OK for someone your age.' None of us wants old hormones in the same way that none of us wants old eyesight. No eye test clinic would send its patients away with the words, 'Your deteriorated eyesight is acceptable for an individual your age.' Instead, they prescribe proper lenses to restore your vision to proper health.

Safe, bio-identical hormones are now compounded in most cities around the world from natural plant-based sources and they are perfect for getting women back to their ideal selves. Bio-identical hormones are different from those used in many traditional hormone replacement therapies (Synthetic HRT), as they are more closely matched to an individual's own personal chemistry, rather than the 'one size fits all' approach using chemicals foreign to the body.

Before you know it, your brain and sleep patterns will be settling back to normal, and your looks, skin tone, vibrancy, mood, sense of well-being and longevity will return. It has been our observation that women who proactively balance their hormones, compared against those who do not, are the ones who do look younger, feel better, function more optimally, regain confidence and live longer.

What Men Don't Get About Hormones

Menopause is most commonly thought of as a life event that happens only to women. You may already know that plummeting hormone levels mean that many women experience sometimes dramatic symptoms, including lack of concentration, irritability, hot flushes, depression and weight gain.

While the female menopause is widely known, there is less awareness of its male counterpart, the andropause. The effects of andropause include a gradual reduction of testosterone.

Testosterone is the chief male hormone and is produced by the Leydig cells located in the testes. It is important not just for sex drive, but also for heart health, maintaining strong bones and muscles, and for promoting positive mood, attitude and sense of well-being.

This reduction happens as a factor of a man's age, but the age in question is not the chronological one measured in years. It is measured instead in overall body health – in other words, a man's *physiological,* or *biological,* age. The ageing of men depends a great deal on physical health, and andropause symptoms are now presenting themselves much earlier in men's lives due to their increasingly unhealthy lifestyles.

Being overweight is a contributor to early ageing for anyone in a leadership role, in part because fat tends to replace muscle around the body, especially when combined with poor diet and lack of activity. Fat cells are 'hot spots' of aromatase activity. Aromatase converts testosterone and its derivative androstenedione to the female hormone oestrone. Thus, male levels of oestrogen tend to increase with age, at the expense of testosterone.

Oestrogen also tends to decrease testosterone production – it's a vicious circle. This is why it's so vitally important to keep up strength training (which stimulates testosterone) and to cut the refined oestrogenic foods out of your diet, such as wheat and unfermented soy. Soy milk and tofu are both high in phytoestrogens, goitrogens (thyroid suppressors) and phytic acid. Healthy levels of testosterone are also linked to better cognitive levels, yet sadly the majority of men are unaware of the importance of their hormonal health, especially as they get older. This is vital in helping them stay at the top of their game, and maintaining a full productive life.

Symptoms of Unhealthy Ageing

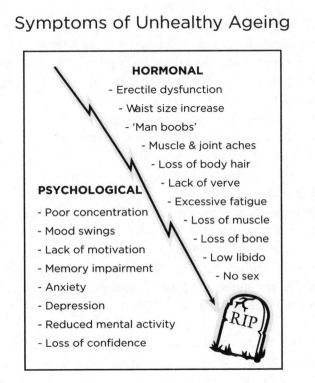

Sexual symptoms include:

»   Suppressed libido
»   Reduction in frequency and quality of sexual activity

In short, getting old badly can really suck. That is, unless you put some effort into fighting it.

'Ageing isn't for sissies.' – Bette Davis

Now, Let's Talk About ED...

While erectile dysfunction (ED) can strike at any time, its incidence increases with age. Half of all men aged between 40 and 70 may be affected.

Dysfunction was once thought to be purely psychological, but the medical pendulum has swung back towards a more physical explanation.

Erectile dysfunction is rather like the canary in the coalmine, and when it occurs it's likely that there could be multiple high-risk factors at play, including atherosclerosis (the build-up of plaque in the arteries), which blocks blood flow to the penis and its capillaries, thus impairing erections. Many associated illnesses are brought on by – you guessed it – excess weight, poor eating habits and lack of exercise.

Don't forget also that the side effects of commonly prescribed drugs account for around 25 per cent of all ED cases. Ironically, given that depression can cause ED, anti-depressant drugs are particularly prone to interfere with sexual functioning.

There's a simple test to check if ED is psychological or physical: if you're still having involuntary or nocturnal erections, it's likely to be a psychological problem, rather than a physical or mechanical one. Here's why. It seems that the normal, non-erect penis requires constant control by the sympathetic nervous system (which regulates involuntary physiological reactions, such as an 'adrenaline rush') to stay flaccid. Sexual stimulation switches off sympathetic control while releasing nitric oxide gas (NO) into the penis. By a complex chemical chain reaction, this relaxes the arteries, which increases blood flow to the spongy tissue in the penis, thus producing an erection.

Erections usually require at least some mental participation but, if the sympathetic system is 'off', spontaneous erections will occur. This happens most often while asleep, particularly during episodes of rapid eye movement (REM) sleep. These nocturnal erections are believed to be a kind of penis maintenance system, but they also serve as a useful diagnostic test for ED. Poor sexual functioning with normal nocturnal erections suggests a psychological, rather than physical, cause. In other words, the problem may be more from the neck up, rather than from the waist down.

Often, however, the causes of ED can be multiple – physiological, psychological and chemical – and one can lead to the other, particularly as men get older. This is why many men need help from the 'little blue pill', even though such drugs can bring as many risks as benefits.

The good news? With a healthy body and clear arteries, you can keep your muscles strong, your hormones regulated, and all your mechanisms, including your penis, functioning correctly and consistently well into your nineties. If you are noticing a lack of morning erections, consider exercising more, provided you have had exercise clearance from a doctor. What most guys don't understand is that small lifestyle changes can do more for your sex life than a load of Viagra and can often decrease the risk of killer diseases as well. Simple changes like losing 4–5kg (10lb), cutting out the after-work drinks, eating quality food, *etc.*, can make a huge difference – plus you will look in great shape and be more attractive too! Don't forget to get your full hormone profiles checked, and then balanced and optimised if they're not in the top 30 per cent of your reference range.

Libido

Our body's relationship with our libido can be likened to a motor vehicle being either finely tuned or experiencing mechanical problems. Both are dependent on having the right combination of fuel, maintenance and usage in order to function optimally.

A healthy sex life has immense benefits for our general health and well-being, but, at some point in our lives, most of us will experience a loss of performance. The hypothalamus in the brain is the hormonal headquarters which, among other things, controls libido and is very sensitive. It is easily affected by fatigue, stress, worry, poor diet, and poor blood flow to the brain and peripheral areas of the body. A common result of many of these conditions is an overwhelming loss of energy.

Men and women are usually made to feel that they themselves are responsible for their own loss of sexual potency, but in actual fact there are a great many external influences at play as well: antihistamines, anti-depressants, beta-blockers, tranquillisers, contraceptive pills, recreational drugs, drinking and smoking have all been shown to impair sexual function, as does diabetes and a string of lifestyle disorders.

The good news is, there is now strong evidence this can be reversed.

Different types of fuels give us the energy needed to take various actions, and some fuels are better than others. For example, energy that comes from exercise and nutritious foods not only fuels you but also supports your long-term health and libido in a positive way. This involves the more frequent consumption of smaller meals that consist of high-quality protein – organic lean red meat, chicken or fish – and lots of vegetables, but without the salt and cheap oils and sauces that restaurants and manufacturers like to add.

Other energy sources, such as alcohol, caffeine, sugar and fast snacks, may deliver intense bursts of power – but they ultimately put your health at risk. Like petrol, you can choose fuel that's slow-burning and lasts over a long time, or you can use the fast-burning rocket fuel, the kind that gives you a powerful immediate boost but burns out quickly. Both types of energy can get certain jobs done, but only one supports your long-term physical and emotional health. One is wise; the other is foolish. Unfortunately, many of us run on the less desirable fuel and end up with bodies, and a love life, which leave us stranded at the side of the road.

To retain and maintain a strong, life-long libido, keep your body fat down and take regular exercise to keep your energy and stamina levels high and your joints supple. Always include weight training to keep your testosterone levels high and, provided there are no injuries, work heavy for maximum benefit.

Wealthy Body Wisdom: Become a student of your own body rather than a passive passenger. Assume control of your own vehicle and you can stay in the driving seat of your performance until you are at least 100 years old.

Sexuality

Sex at any age is part of a normal healthy life. It's also important as we age to keep the fires of youthful hormones burning.

Sadly, many surveys of busy mature executives ranked their sex life somewhere between 'yawn' and 'awful'. And that was the ones who were honest! People who have frequent sex live longer than those who don't. In fact, a study in the *British Medical Journal* found that men who had sex less than once per month were twice as likely to die in the next 10 years than those who had sex once per week. In addition, a 25-year study of 270 men and women aged 60 to 96 conducted at Duke University found that the more men had sex, the longer they lived, and women who said they enjoyed their sex lives lived seven to eight years longer than those who were indifferent.

Many men and women blame their age or their relationship for problems with their sex lives, when actually it could be due to a hormonal imbalance.

A growing waistline, loss of muscle, lack of energy, mood swings and snoring can be attributed to a lowering of the hormone testosterone.

One reason for this may be that many middle-aged and older adults are taking medications and not realising that side effects can negatively impact their sexual performance or enjoyment.

A human's sexuality is as essential to overall health as all the other body systems, and is an integral part of attaining The Wealthy Body.

Here's the thing: when a person's heart or pancreas stops working, they take this very seriously, and will often seek treatment.

But when the sexual system no longer works properly, this is considered a non-event, even a rite of passage.

Do not buy into this! Besides activating your hormonal system, sexuality is vital for self-esteem, confidence and is part of a healthy lifestyle, just like exercise and nutritious food.

Wealthy Body Wisdom: Don't be afraid of hormone replacement. If you want to operate at a higher level in business and look younger, you need to get to grips with your hormones. So why accept the same approach with your hormones? If they are deteriorating, seek some corrective action! Hormone disruption is not just some stage you suddenly go through when you hit a certain age. It starts much earlier and it is important to be thoroughly briefed on it and the options available. Sometimes your *doctor isn't the best person to do this and may refer you. Hormones are the master organisers within the body, influencing all systems, and when they function properly within our 24-hour cycles we operate at our very best. Find a bio-identical hormone specialist doctor for natural treatment. You will feel 10 years younger!*

9.
EXERCISE –
THE BRAIN-BODY
CONNECTION

To keep the business brain operating at peak performance, your body needs to work hard.

If you can get to the point where you're consistently saying to yourself that exercise is something you want to do, then you are charting a course to a very different future – one that's less about surviving as you age and more about thriving.

It has been known for a long time that exercise increases levels of serotonin, norepinephrine and dopamine – all of which are important neurotransmitters that help move signals, thoughts and emotions through the brain.

> *Sit-ups don't burn fat. You would have to complete 250,000 consecutive sit-ups to burn less than half a kilo (1lb) of fat.*

And although we know exercise unleashes a cascade of neurochemicals and growth factors bolstering the brain's infrastructure, still it is under-utilised.

The brain responds like all living systems, growing with use, or atrophying with inactivity. The neurons in the brain connect to one another through 'leaves' on treelike branches, and exercise causes those branches to be stimulated and grow, thus enhancing brain function at a fundamental level.

Neuroscientists have only just begun to study the full impact of exercise within brain cells – and at the level of genes themselves. Even there, in the roots of our biology, they've found signs of the body's influence on the mind.

It turns out that moving muscles produce proteins that travel through the bloodstream and into the brain, where they play pivotal roles in the mechanisms of our highest thought processes.

They bear names such as insulin-like growth factor (IGF-1) and vascular endothelial growth factor (VEGF), and they provide an unprecedented view of the mind-body connection. It's only in the past few years that neuroscientists have begun to describe these factors and how they work, and each new discovery adds awe-inspiring depth to the picture.

> **Wealthy Body Wisdom:** Lifting weights can make you smarter! Muscles forced to grow and become stronger create new neural connections in the brain, increasing overall brain activity and growth.

There's still much we don't understand about what happens in the microenvironment of the brain, but what we do know can change people's lives.

Why should you care about how your brain works? For one thing, it's running the show, it's the master computer. As you read this book, the frontal area of your brain is firing signals about what you're reading, and how much of it you soak up has a lot to do with whether there is a proper balance of neurochemicals and growth factors to bind neurons together.

Exercise has a documented, dramatic effect on these essential processes. It sets the stage, and when you sit down to learn something new, the stimulation of exercise strengthens the relevant connections. With practice, the circuit develops definition, just as if you're wearing down a path through a forest.

The importance of making these connections carries over to all of the areas in your body. In order to cope with anxiety, for instance, you need to let certain well-worn paths grow over while you blaze new, alternate trails.

By understanding such interactions between your body and your brain, you can manage the process, handle problems and get your mind humming along smoothly.

> *Wealthy Body Wisdom: If you had exercised for an hour this morning, you would now be in a better frame of mind to sit still and focus on this page. Your brain would be far better equipped to remember and use the information you have just read.*

If you have been suffering from emotional conditions such as excessive worry, depression or lethargy, a first step out of the darkness and back towards the light of a normal, fulfilled life is to recognise a lot of the cause is in fact biological. Yes, there may be circumstances in your life (pressure, balance, relationships, etc.) that are the cause of your discomfort, but its manifestation and agony is in great part physiological, and can be cured by a combination of activity, nutrition, rest and recovery, and hormone optimisation.

Physical activity has been shown to be better than chemical medications, such as sertraline (Zoloft), for treating depression.[16]

Unfortunately, exercise comes disguised as hard work. It cannot be patented or owned by large pharmaceutical companies or multi-nationals, who are keen to offer instead the promise of a less arduous path.

It is easier, it seems, to take a pill than to lift a dumbbell.

And that's a shame, because so many cures, both reactive and preventative, exist within the complex chemistry of the human body itself.

You can influence your physiology. You can change your life.

Wealthy Body Fact: An experiment, described in USA Today *(September 21, 2005), took a group of literacy students and observed their academic performance on tests at different periods following exercise. One class took the test immediately following exercise, and the other approximately six hours later. The class that took the tests immediately after exercise consistently performed better. The results of this test, and many more like it, spread beyond freshmen who simply need to boost their reading scores. It has implications in terms of improved studying strategies, such as scheduling the hardest subjects immediately after going to the gym, to capitalise on the beneficial effects of exercise.*

And these concepts apply not only to the academic world but equally importantly in the business world. Would you not want and expect peak performance from yourself and your team? When do you think that would best be attained? Before or after exercise? And how can you factor exercise into an office environment. It can be done. It's a matter of challenging convention and recognising that your body and mind react best when they re looked after.

Committing to Staying Fit

Nobody is too busy to get fit. As a recent article in *Forbes* magazine (January 3, 2013) pointed out, the most successful CEOs of the most successful companies are committed to staying in great physical shape so that they stay in great mental shape. Just like Richard Branson, mentioned earlier, they recognise that the secret to great leadership and great achievement comes from working the entire body. Here are some other examples:

» When John Chambers was CEO of Cisco, he jogged five miles (8km) a day.

» Colm Kelleher, President of Morgan Stanley, trains hard 5–6 days a week, and maintains a trim, athletic physique. 'Obviously observing a high-performance diet is a key part of the overall regime,' he says.

» Apple CEO Tim Cook is a fitness buff: working out, hiking and cycling, he says he is the most energetic person in the room, even after a 12-hour flight.
» Former US President Barack Obama still works out early every morning and enjoys pick-up basketball games.

The commitment comes from recognising the benefits of the exercise, not its drawbacks.

Wealthy Body Wisdom: The time spent exercising is not wasted or lost. It is an investment in energy.

How to Avoid Falling Off the Exercise Wagon? Variety!

There is a commonly held belief that a challenging exercise routine is not normal, that it is only for the budding athlete or 'health nut', and that a walk in the park is all the average person needs to stay in great shape.

This is incorrect.

Genetically, humans were designed to be lean, fit and extremely physical. In the hunter-gatherer days of millions of years ago, food was scarcer but its overall quality was three times more nutritious.

If you are losing energy by 3 p.m. ... you've blown it!

There are many different opinions as to what optimal fitness for health actually is. Some people believe they are fit and healthy because they live a busy life; others believe that they are doing alright because they walk everywhere. Some people think a slim body is an indication of fitness, or that good health is just absence of sickness or disease.

Now, these are all important individual contributors to the concept of fitness for health, but they are only a part of the whole.

The secret that so many fail to understand as they doggedly stick to only one or two disciplines, is that just like food, it is *variety* that makes for healthy fitness.

Fitness for optimal health consists of *four* essential components. Just as a seat requires four legs to be functional and stable, all are equally important because they intrinsically link and interact with each other!

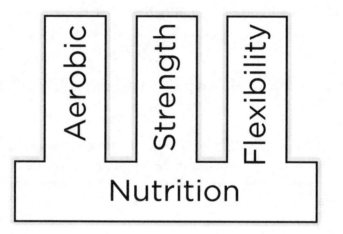

1. Aerobic Fitness

The benefits of aerobic fitness start with the heart. This is the measure of the heart's ability to pump oxygen-rich blood around the body to organs and the working muscles. An unfit heart is like the engine of a small car, labouring under a heavy load. It makes you puff when you bound upstairs or dash to catch the bus. A healthy, trained heart is like swapping that motor for a high-powered V8. It will pump greater volumes of blood around your body with each stroke, giving you increased energy.

2. Muscle Strength

You can be aerobically fit, but not strong or toned. Muscle tone is definitely not just for body-builders and Charles Atlas-types. The muscles of the body can be likened to a corset holding the body's internal organs firm and shapely, while also providing support for the bones to give good posture. Many an older person has been confined into care or into a wheelchair, not necessarily because they are sick, but just because they are *weak*.

Strong, toned muscles also keep you free from imbalances that can lead to everyday injuries.

Muscles also play a fantastic role in weight loss because they require a lot of energy and are greedy calorie burners.

They are also key players in keeping your hormones stable and, when in a state of growth, stimulate the production of important anti-ageing growth hormones, and the release of endorphins.

> **Wealthy Body Wisdom:** *A combination of both aerobic fitness and muscle strength is essential. Otherwise you might be aerobically fit but not strong, or strong but not fit.*

3. Flexibility

Functional flexibility of the muscles, ligaments and tendons around all your joints is vital for good posture, balance and mobility. The renowned strength guru Charles Poliquin says, 'One of the key factors inhibiting muscle growth potential is restricted range of motion.' Lack of flexibility in specific areas will leave the body prone to injury and pain, which gradually increases with age. Muscle tightness can also destroy your posture, creating a stooped, hunched or collapsed frame.

4. Nutrition

Once again, fitness is never complete without good nutrition, and good nutrition is never complete without the right exercise. One is never more important than the other.

To improve performance, to get fitter or to lose fat, exercise works on an overload principle; this states that extra stress must be placed regularly on all the structures within the body for improvement, maintenance and repair of its functions. For this to happen successfully we need to supply superior levels of nutrition to send the raw materials the body needs. Too often the uninformed exerciser trains long and hard, while at the same time severely restricting food intake to lose weight. This is completely counterproductive, unhealthy, and a total waste of time.

Fitness Myths and Myth-information

Are the scales a correct measure of body composition?
No. Not at all. Based on bodyweight alone, the average adult changes 10lb per decade but based on body composition they actually change 20lb per decade. 5lb less of muscle and 15lb more of fat… The scales never tell the whole story!

What body fat percentage does an average man need to have a six pack?
It differs from person to person. But usually he needs to get down somewhere under 10 per cent body fat before the abs really begin to 'show' themselves. For a woman, it's a little higher – around 15 per cent. The more toned and developed they are, the better, but they will stand out the same as a man's.

I eat healthy but can't seem to lose weight.
We hear this all the time. If you were eating healthy you would be your ideal weight! Remember, simply not eating junk, doesn't mean you're eating healthy in the same way that simply not being bankrupt, doesn't mean you're wealthy… Eating healthy means that everything you put in your mouth will, in some way, advance your health position. Even if it's healthy food, if you eat too much and store some of it as fat – that may not be healthy for you.

If I've been trying everything and I'm not losing weight, is there any point in carrying on exercising?
A good bout of exercise reduces stress and helps keep the arteries clear.

Exercise also makes the detoxification cycle run faster in the body, keeping the brain clearer and improving liver insulin sensitivity. (Not if you keep drinking alcohol regularly, though!) The psychological benefits of a good workout have always proven to give relief to both depression and anxiety. Check your diet, as weight loss will happen when both of these lifestyle habits are in place together. Remember, gaining The Wealthy Body is the whole package!

People often say you gain energy after you exercise. Even though I work out often, it doesn't make me feel energetic. Is there a reason why?
You need quality, natural whole food to give you the exercise energy. There may also be another problem – for example, adrenal fatigue or thyroid irregularities. If you're over 40, have your hormones checked, balanced and optimised.

Once I lose weight will I still have to eat like this?
Those who fail to make permanent lifestyle changes get only temporary results. Stay with it, as you will increase your health and longevity as well. If you go back to your old ways you will return to your old figure. There needs to be a permanent change in habits, attitude, thinking, eating and activities. Remember our golden rule: 'You can't have a lean body and a fat head.'

I hate running to get the required 30 minutes of cardio in.
Do what you enjoy and it won't be a chore. Try shorter sprints, take different classes, run the stairs 10 times, skip, cycle, boxercise, row, play regular sports...

And Finally...

Become an expert on your own physique. People who get results don't quit. There will be inconveniences and obstacles that seem to get in the way, but the challenged and the successful always get to their goal in spite of these. Keep yourself updated and be interested in the latest news and research topics on fitness and health. Read everything possible – not the latest fad diet and sensationalist exercise routines from celebrities or models, but articles written by athletes, coaches and independent researchers. After all, athletes don't starve themselves to look good.

There is a proliferation of information available everywhere today, but often the vital ingredient missing is the sustained input of an experienced, successful coach being with you until your knowledge becomes a habit.

Clients who have taken the time to take care of themselves have found improvements in other areas of their lives as well, including relationships, careers, self-esteem, confidence, hobbies and sporting abilities. Our reputation is built upon results that come from positive action, so anybody can enjoy that special confidence and self-reliance that comes from being in control of your own physiology. The decision you take now to repair, improve and age-proof your physique is a commitment and an investment in your health, wealth and future. It could be the best money you have ever spent in your life. That's why we call it The Wealthy Body.

So, value your body – and invest in your future.

10.
CREATING THE
WEALTHY BODY

Exercising to lose weight or to stay fit is an admirable goal. But there are many dangers associated with doing that solely through aerobic or endurance training.

The commonly held belief is that you should do 45 minutes to an hour or more a day of aerobic activity. However, this has led to an over-trained, flabby, immune-compromised population of exercisers.

This is because once you become fit enough to perform the activity you're doing, but don't change or increase the intensity or workload – it remains at a constant steady state and your body adapts to that exercise to become more efficient at it. This means it becomes less effective at burning fat and stimulating muscle growth.

What's missing is intensity – and intensity requires power, speed and strength.

We see men and women, season after season, plodding the streets, swimming the lanes or pounding the treadmills, but getting very little in payback. This is largely because they're doing the same thing they've always done, and at a level of intensity that fails to maintain muscle homeostasis.

Aerobic exercise *is* important, but unless you throw some power, speed and strength work in the mix, it won't stop people getting weaker as they age.

Extended steady-state, aerobic-only training also causes you to lose muscle, and go from a big apple to a small apple, from a big pear to a small pear … if you're lucky.

This is because we are not designed to run for long periods without the extra conditioning provided by high-intensity strength and power activities – lifting, climbing, sprinting, pushing, dragging, fighting, throwing.

There are many physical issues caused by doing steady-state endurance training to the exclusion of strength:

> » depletion of lean muscle tissue
> » suppression and imbalance of key growth hormones

- » suppressed metabolic function
- » osteoarthritis, even at a younger age
- » tendonitis and other repetitive strain injuries
- » increased oxidative damage (free radical production)
- » susceptibility to injury and to infections
- » loss of bone density

The days of only doing aerobics to achieve fitness are long gone.

Why then do some people charge into their senior years being active, mobile, alert and fun until the end, yet others labour their way through later life becoming ever more weak, fragile and sick?

Staying *strong* and optimally nourished is the answer!

It is *weakness* that robs women and men of their youth.

Firing Up Your Metabolism

Y N	Do you find that you can't eat as much as you used to without getting fat?
Y N	Does it seem that you have less energy than you used to?
Y N	Are you not as strong as you used to be?
Y N	Do you ever say, *I know I should exercise, but don't have the energy*?
Y N	Do you feel tired and worn-out at the end of a normal day?
Y N	Do you feel tired and worn-out at the *start* of a normal day?
Y N	Do you feel older than your years?
Y N	Do you ever look at older relatives and wonder if this will be you in years to come?

These problems all have a simple explanation: sarcopenia (atrophied muscles).

Muscles shrink as you age. An efficient muscle is like an efficient car engine. Toned, active muscles burn calories, even if idle. But if you have less muscle, this causes your metabolism to slow.

Your metabolism slows each decade, starting in the mid-twenties, and this loss accelerates as you age, depending on your lifestyle.

So, it stands to reason that if, through exercising in the right way, you can slow or stop this muscle loss, you can keep your metabolism as speedy as it was when you were younger. Target training your muscle has many benefits.

Myth: Am I too old to lift weights with the expectation of getting stronger?

A: Nope. People of all ages should weight train. We are always surprised by the lack of older people working out in gyms in the UK. When we do see them, they are usually bobbing gently about in the pool or swishing aimlessly away on the cardio machines.

There is overwhelming evidence that we start losing muscle from the early age of 25, and this accelerates as we age. Along with this muscle loss comes physical weakness and an increase in body fat to nearly double by the age of 60.

Older people need to weight train with more urgency and verve than younger people – and it's never too late to start. Research shows that older people who weight train experience less knee pain, more joint strength and significantly less depression than those who don't.[17]

Your body doesn't own a clock – you can feel young at any age.

Myth: Weight training will give women big muscles.

A: It is time for this old wives' tale to die. Gaining muscle mass for most women is extremely hard. In fact, you *wouldn't believe what you would have to go through to gain extreme muscle size. Even just to get back, and maintain, normal functional muscle requires diligent strength training, strict adherence to nutrition, and adequate rest and recovery – you will have to work at it in order to fight the destructive effects of age.*

The beauty of it is, the more muscle you have on your body, the more fat you burn when you exercise – and even when you don't! Better to have some shape and firmness to your body, and muscle on your arms, than muffin tops and bingo wings!

Helping Balance Your Hormones

Scientists have found that long-term weight training increases the production of human growth hormone (HGH), Dehydroepiandrosterone (DHEA) and insulin-like growth factor IGF-1 – your anti-ageing hormones.

Researchers are just beginning to understand the importance of HGH, which is made in the pea-sized pituitary gland at the base of the skull. In women growth hormone has an important role in retaining muscle tone and bone density, for which men rely more on testosterone.

Growth hormone helps fight general tissue breakdown, which also improves many metabolic functions including weight control.

Growth hormone is responsive to heavier exercise regimes of 3–8 repetitions when weight training.

Keep this as part of your exercise routine and you can eliminate many of the markers of ageing – poor posture, a thickening waist, languishing libido, wrinkling knees, wobbly jowls and a general loss of energy.

Lowering Your Blood Sugar

As muscle mass shrinks, blood sugar levels can increase even if you don't have diabetes.

By age 70, an increasing number of men and women have an abnormally high level of sugar in the blood after a big meal.

Why is the sugar level higher?

Well, muscle is the primary location where the body puts the sugar you eat in the form of glycogen. If you're active, that sugar is burned by muscle immediately or is stored as reserve fuel. If you're sedentary, the excess sugar is circulated back to the liver and converted into fat.

Also, as a person becomes fatter and less muscular, insulin (the hormone that regulates blood sugar) doesn't work so well. So as you get older, fatter and less muscular, your blood sugar will rise.

The problem with high blood sugar is it's inflammatory and high acid – both conditions that cause and contribute to cardiovascular disease, so maintaining normal levels is crucial for your longevity prospects.

In your whole blood supply there is usually just over 1 teaspoon of sugar at any one time, so you can see how even a small increase can affect the natural balances dramatically.

You can use an inexpensive blood sugar meter to test your blood sugar levels yourself at home. You do not need a prescription to buy the meter or strips, which you can get from your local pharmacy.

What's a normal measurement? If taken randomly during the day, it should be below 11.1mmol/l (millimoles per litre) or 200mg/dl (milligrams per decilitre). If taken after fasting, readings should be below 6.1mmol/l or 108mg/dl.

If you're not sure, ask your doctor, who may want to commission a more comprehensive blood sample test.

Don't Take the Batteries Out...

I happened to have a conversation with an old friend, Steve, recently. In fact he's one of the original members who joined our first health club nearly 25 years ago in Timaru, New Zealand. He's still in terrific shape, and maintains a rigorous schedule of exercise and quality nutrition. He's also Type 2 diabetic, meaning he has to be very careful to manage his lifestyle, and regularly checks and monitors his blood glucose and insulin functions.

But not everybody does.

'Just yesterday I was having a cup of tea in town with a group of people,' Steve told me. 'One woman was there eating an enormous cream bun. I leaned in and said to her quietly, "I thought you had diabetes, Helen." She replied, "Yes, but I'm on insulin now, so it's all under control." I said, "Are you sure? I have my test kit on me. Would you like me to check your numbers for you?" She reluctantly agreed, and I performed a quick finger prick test. Imagine my surprise when her blood sugar count came in at over 22, although *surprise* is not the word for it. I was more saddened. This woman was going to die, and it was not her diabetes that would kill her, but her ignorance. Just because you're handed a management strategy for your symptoms, doesn't give you permission to bury your head in the sand when it comes to your behaviours. What do you think?'

I thought for a moment before replying because I know many people have offered the same argument when I've discussed this in our seminars and workshops. Finally I said, 'I agree – that mindset is based on folly. It's like taking the batteries out of a smoke alarm to stop the piercing noise. Your family can all go back to sleep, but your kitchen is still burning down.'

Reducing Stress and Strengthening Your Frame

Weight-lifting is one of the best ways to naturally improve mood. It reduces stress, anxiety and depression[18], and creates a sense of happiness.

If you're stressed, feeling irritable or low, simply do a quick, intense workout. Like a runner's high, this stimulates endorphin production.

Researchers have found that light to moderate weight training or cardiovascular exercise doesn't produce nearly as many endorphins as heavy weight training or training that incorporates sprinting or other anaerobic exertion. Again, it's *intensity* that ensures results.

Don't be put off; the level at which this will be set is always based on your own level of strength fitness. It will literally make you feel 100 times better.

Working out against significant resistance also increases bone weight and density more effectively than cycling, swimming or jogging.[19] A *balanced* strength-training programme loads most major bones in the body, which makes them adapt, thus offering protection against osteoporosis. A person at any age can do it. It is not just for the young, or for fitness junkies.

Remember this too: there is no better solution to the slouch-shouldered, potbellied, bent-over look of a person approaching middle age than an increase in muscle mass. Poor posture is ageing!

Strong Leaders Stay Young!

Every decade, you lose muscle. This may not be particularly noticeable, because fat often replaces the space and weight previously occupied by your muscle.

The average 35-year-old man is 18 per cent fat, but by age 65, he's 38 per cent fat, and in many cases weighs the same, or less! The less muscle you have, the less you can eat without getting fat, since you have less active tissue to burn calories at rest and during exercise.

It's a 'use it or lose it' phenomenon.

Wealthy Body Wisdom: In a major announcement made in July 2011 the American College of Sports Medicine (ACSM) now recommends weight training for every adult.

Wealthy Body Wisdom: The courage to make intelligent choices is like a muscle – the more it is used, the stronger it becomes.

11.
UNDERSTANDING HOMOCYSTEINE, THE BIO-MARKER

It was about 5 o'clock on a balmy summer afternoon in Hampstead, London, and I'd just arrived at a client's house to conduct his regular fortnightly assessment. This one was significant, as it marked Andrew's final, benchmark measure-up.

I deftly ran the tape around his trimmed and rebuilt frame, followed closely by body fat calliper measurements. We also ran through his fitness, strength and agility tests before checking his 'medical' markers, as I like to call them.

Blood pressure was great, heart pattern on the ECG was fine, and as a final test we did a droplet blood test for homocysteine, which I promptly sent off to the lab.

I'm pleased to report that Andrew achieved 3 out of 3 for the targets we had set at the start of his programme – one of the small percentage of clients who have done so. (The targets we set with our clients are always fair and achievable, but by no means easy!) However, when I received his homocysteine report back from the lab about two weeks later, I was shocked.

Instead of getting better, as I had predicted, they were worse! Andrew's initial reading was 11 on the scale (ideal is between 5 and 7). Now, despite losing weight, getting fit, completely overhauling his diet and recording improvement on all his other bio-markers, Andrew had increased his 'H' score to nearly 19!

Something was clearly wrong, so I advised Andrew to seek medical opinion and perhaps submit to more in-depth testing.

Upon investigation, it turned out that my client had the very early stages of bladder cancer, which fortunately was caught in time. After many months of treatment and therapy, Andrew came through with a clean bill of health – much to everyone's relief.

Subsequent testing proved satisfactory, as homocysteine scores dropped back down into the normal range, and have remained so ever since. There has been no further sign of the cancer.

When we work with our executive clients, we like to start with a homocysteine blood test.[20]

Homocysteine is an amino acid produced in the human body by the chemical conversion of methionine, a compound regularly consumed within the diet. It is toxic and is found in blood plasma when the body's chemistry is out of balance.

Homocysteine is a strong and reliable marker for imbalance, inflammation and presence of other diseases in the body. Andrew's case was a reminder to us all that getting regular medical checks is an essential health strategy as we age.

Many medical experts and scientific studies around the world, including the British Cardiac Patients Association, are now hailing homocysteine as a better predictor of potential health problems than cholesterol levels.

This is because homocysteine is a major indicator for heart attacks, coronary heart disease and one of the best predictors of Alzheimer's and most other nervous system disorders. These silent diseases remain the biggest killers in the Western world. In the UK they account for around 125,000 deaths a year – approximately one in four deaths in men, and one in six in women.

Your homocysteine level is the best single indicator of whether you are going to live a long and healthy life, or suffer problems at a younger age. A high homocysteine reading has been directly linked to, and in many cases is the cause of, over 100 conditions including:

» Alzheimer's and early-onset dementia
» cerebral atrophy (brain shrinkage)
» pregnancy problems and birth defects
» memory deficit
» depression
» schizophrenia
» arthritis
» cancer
» chronic fatigue
» diabetes
» heart attacks
» infertility

- » obesity
- » accelerated ageing
- » strokes
- » thyroid problems
- » ulcers
- » deep vein thrombosis (DVT)
- » headaches

Fifty per cent of deaths are due to preventable diseases, and one in every two has a high homocysteine level. Coincidence...?

Your homocysteine level (also called your H-Level) tells whether you are doing enough to keep yourself in tip-top condition.

High-risk groups include people who smoke, have an unbalanced diet, are stressed, have a family history of disease, have a high consumption of alcohol (more than two glasses a day), who exercise infrequently and who are overweight (body fat of 20 per cent or more in men, 25 per cent or more in women) or carry a lot of weight around the abdomen. H-levels can also increase with age, oestrogen deficiency and with some medications.

How High is Too High?

Optimum levels have been suggested as less than a score of 6, with 6–9 being low risk, 9–15 being high risk, and scores over 15 rated as very high risk.

If your score is higher than 10, you can be sure that there will be at least some degree of cerebral volume loss – or brain shrinkage.

Current research has indicated that an increase in homocysteine ratings of just 5 points showed a 32–42 per cent increase in risk for heart disease, a 60 per cent increase in risk for Deep Vein Thrombosis (DVT) and a 59–65 per cent increase in risk for stroke.[21]

A high level of homocysteine in the blood is toxic to the vascular system and damages and thickens the walls of the arteries. Homocysteine doesn't just cause artery damage – a high accumulation reduces the body's effectiveness in producing vital biochemicals that reduce your risk of a variety of conditions and diseases. It is also toxic and damaging to the nerve cells, especially brain neurons but also motor and pain response nerves.

There are high-risk groups and low-risk groups, but the best way for you to find out is to have a test. Whatever your state-of-health, a homocysteine test will let you know what your risk is.

Getting a test is easy, and you can order a simple home test kit online, complete the test at home (a fingerprick droplet of blood is all that's required), and send it off in the mail to the lab. In the UK we use Lorisian (www.lorisian.com), a division of YorkTest labs.

The good news is, high H-levels can be reduced in a relatively short time with the right nutrients and the right changes in lifestyle.

Homocysteine busters include:

Eating less processed meat, more fish and vegetable protein

Cutting back on coffee and caffeinated drinks. Drinking two shots of coffee can raise homocysteine levels by as much as 11 per cent within two hours

Cutting back on alcohol and sugar

Reducing your stress levels

Stopping smoking

Supplementing your diet with homocysteine-lowering nutrients daily: folate; vitamins b12, b6 and b2; zinc and magnesium. Vegetarians and vegans can also be at risk of higher H-levels, since some of the best sources of these are found in animal products

Taking regular exercise, of course

Because of the change in eating habits of our modern Western world, over half the population in the UK currently fails to get even the minimum requirement of these vitamins. As well as causing a rise in homocysteine levels, these deficiencies are instrumental in creating unreasonable fatigue and stress, irritability, carbohydrate craving, PMT and depression. B6 is also vital in creating a strong antioxidant and detoxifying effect within the body, important for a strong immune system and warding off the winter colds and the flu.

The bottom line: a raised homocysteine score, especially when significantly raised, is never good, as it suggests a deficiency in B-vitamins, the presence of serious underlying disease, and/or an unhealthy lifestyle.

For men and women wanting to achieve The Wealthy Body, there is clear benefit in lowering elevated homocysteine levels to reduce risk of early-onset disease.

Wealthy Body Action Points

1. To increase your intake of B-group vitamins, load more dark leafy greens on your plate – such as spinach, kale and chard – and more seafood and beef (B12).

2. Increase magnesium and zinc levels by eating nuts and seeds in small amounts. Seeds (which includes nuts) are tremendously valuable because they contain concentrated nutrients – about 20- to 30-fold more than the rest of the fruit or plant they come from. They contain the blueprint for growth, with all sorts of genetic spare parts that can help repair DNA and RNA. They also have tremendous stem cell precursors, especially the husk of the seeds. Great seeds to include in your everyday diet include quinoa, chia and sunflower seeds (especially sprouted). The best nuts to eat are Brazils, almonds, walnuts and pumpkin seeds.

3. Include a clove of garlic in your diet every day, as it is known to have anti-inflammatory and anti-viral properties.

4. Supplement with a high-quality, whole-food multi-vitamin/mineral.

Wealthy Body Wisdom: *The colours in fruits and vegetables reflect the differing unique phytochemicals and antioxidants they contain. Eat a large colour range of vegetables to protect your body against oxidation, inflammation and all the ageing diseases.*

Myth: I need to drink coffee during the day to stay sharp and on top of things.

A: Let's be very clear about this. Coffee, black tea and caffeine-based energy drinks, will certainly pick up brain speed and reaction time – no question. There are, however, other issues to take into account.

Caffeine-based energy drinks are often combined with massive amounts of sugar and other chemicals, with which your body struggles to cope. Even a skinny cappuccino has about 100 calories of sugar from the lactose in the milk, and often goes hand-in-hand with other high-sugar, empty-nutrition snacks (muffins, pastries, chocolate, etc.).

From the perspective of business performance, a more important side effect is that caffeine raises the stress hormone cortisol. Raised cortisol has the effect of suppressing your main alpha-drive hormone, testosterone – which is responsible for mood, confidence, immunity and bone density among other things.

In the long term, elevated cortisol will overload your adrenal glands leading to adrenal fatigue (see below), damage thyroid function, shorten attention span, slow the speed at which you process information, and affect short-term memory. Unfortunately, habitual use of stimulants always has downsides and these eventually drain your energy, damage your health and slow the business brain.

Adrenal Fatigue

The basis of adrenal fatigue or burnout is stress, which over time can tax your adrenal glands to the point of causing symptoms, such as sleep disorders, weight gain, chronic fatigue and depression.

The precipitating event for most people is a period of intense emotional stress.

Conventionally, if you suspect you're suffering from over-taxed or worn-out adrenals, you'd see your GP or perhaps an endocrinologist who would evaluate your adrenal glands. Unfortunately, they tend to primarily test for specific diseases like Addison's Disease (where the body under-produces cortisol) or Cushing's Syndrome (over-production of cortisol), both of which are relatively rare.

What isn't always considered is that both are extreme medical conditions, and not what most people suffer from, therefore conventional tests may not reveal the underlying problem.

There is, however, a valuable lab test called a "Functional Adrenal Stress Profile', which shifts the investigation from qualifying a possible disease to identifying functional problems. These may not be severe enough to require hospitalisation, but can certainly impact personal and professional functional capacity. Symptoms may include fatigue, depression, problems with weight gain, and problems with sleep.

The tests are very simple to administer and involve collection of either saliva or urine samples.

Renowned adrenal expert Dr Daniel Kalish is the designer of the Kalish Method for treating adrenal disorders.

The Kalish Method* calls for testing your adrenal function by taking four saliva (or urine) samples over the course of a day. These map out your circadian rhythm, showing how your cortisol levels rise and fall over a 24-hour period. This information is evaluated and restorative protocols put in place to correct and reset cortisol production. In the first instance this would include establishing a consistent exercise programme, avoiding stimulant drinks and sugary foods, and striving for better sleep, rest and recovery habits.

What's also interesting about the adrenals is their connection to the thyroid. As the cortisol levels go up, one of the normal body mechanisms is to down-regulate the thyroid, so most people with high cortisol are going to have lower than ideal thyroid hormone levels. An adrenal restoration programme may be enough to restore normal thyroid function.

---

* http:/kalishwellness.com

12.
DEPRESSED? EAT YOUR WAY OUT!

When you're moody or depressed, you probably don't look to balance your diet or take a multi-vitamin to decrease your symptoms.

This modern disease is becoming one of the biggest burdens on our society, according to the World Health Organization, and a great many key earners suffer from this silently.

A recent study published in the *American Journal of Clinical Nutrition*[22] found that over-consumption of refined carbohydrates and sugars was associated with greater odds of depression. But some aspects of dietary intake also had *positive* effects against depression, including fibre, whole grains, whole fruits and vegetables.

A high-glycaemic diet also increased risk for inflammation and cardio-vascular disease – both precursors to the development of depression. In addition, this type of diet also led to increased insulin resistance, which, in turn, led to cognitive deficits mirroring those found in people with mood disorders and depression.

Statistics show that as many as one in three people feel depressed and suffer from low moods. This is why millions of people are prescribed anti-depressants. Yet the long-term side effects of many of these drugs can be depressing in themselves, with a list that includes:

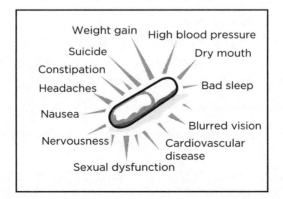

What many people aren't aware of is that there is a much simpler, more natural way of dealing with the imbalances that lead to depression: food.

Now it is important here to distinguish between reactive comfort food, such as ice cream and crisps, and proactive anti-depressant foods.

Part of the reason people reach for the ice cream when they feel depressed is because the body knows that ice cream and other so-called comfort foods contain sugar and fat. When the body is stressed, it reacts out of fear. It interprets the stress being felt as a signal that food is scarce (a basic primordial fear), and therefore looks for sources of food to store for the anticipated famine to come. This reaction, combined with the Western world's abundance of high-fat, high-sugar foods, makes it easy to reach for and find comfort.

The reason why these foods feel so good is that they are answering an instinctive call. But sadly, they are the wrong foods. They are stand-ins for the good, energy-rich but pollutant-free meals that no longer exist.

Your metabolism is being conned at its weakest moment.

What has been made clear from all current studies is that the best ways of banishing the blues for good includes top mood- and mind-boosting nutrients and supplements, and getting the biochemistry right before turning to medication. This is because the most effective and safest way of altering the brain's complex biochemistry is with the stuff that it is actually made of – the food you eat. The brain is the most chemically sensitive organ in the body and it is often treated as if it were separate to the rest of the body. But it's not.

How to Boost Your Mood and Drive

1. Cut Out the Stimulants

A diet too high in sugar and stimulants (coffee, tea, nicotine, sports drinks, energy drinks, fruit juice, chocolate bars, candy) will upset your blood sugar and make you more prone to emotional ups and downs.

> **Wealthy Body Wisdom:** High performance doesn't come in a coffee cup.

2. Cut Out the Depressants

Alcohol is a depressant, and is used to self-medicate, sometimes to extreme excess. An alcoholic binge fills the body with poisons, dehydrates it, and robs the wallet of money. And the problems are still there once the hangover clears.

Is there any type of alcohol that is acceptable?

We attend many cocktail parties and work functions. Alcohol is a neurotoxin, diuretic, depressant, hormone disruptor and a caloric bomb. Many non-drinkers and recovering alcoholics survive fine in a social environment. Have one glass of champagne and then keep your glass topped up with sparkling water. This can be done also with half and half grape or grapefruit juice. Nobody will know if you don't tell them!

Once you've got the stimulants and depressants out of your system, you'll be surprised at how easy it is to live without them. If you have been drinking coffee or tea regularly for some time, you might want to cut down gradually to avoid caffeine-withdrawal headaches. However, once you're off them, you'll notice a marked difference in your mood and energy. A great way to do this is to substitute with green or nettle tea. Keep coffee or tea around for special occasions when they won't have such an effect on your health.

3. Balance Your Blood Sugar With Chromium

Most people are vastly deficient in chromium. Chromium is found in whole grains, seafood, green beans, broccoli, prunes and potatoes, so as well as taking an extra supplement, eat these foods when you want a boost. It will also help you lose weight. You can also try adding cinnamon to drinks and meals, as it has been shown in studies to reduce both blood glucose and cholesterol levels.

The eminent nutrition guru, Patrick Holford advises that people who are finding it difficult to give up sugar should try supplementing up to 600mg of chromium a day, 400mg with breakfast and 200mg with lunch. Chromium is fantastic for banishing sugar cravings. It is a natural anti-depressant and a very important nutrient to include in your mood-boosting diet.

4. Eat Enough Protein

Having a serving of lean meat, fish, chicken, turkey, eggs, fermented soy (tempeh, miso or natto) or protein powder (added to your smoothie) each day can add important amino acids. These are the building blocks of protein and are known to help give your brain a natural mood boost.

5. Get Hold of Some Tryptophan

This is the amino acid that helps manufacture the feel-good neurotransmitter serotonin. It is one of nature's most effective pick-me-ups. Tryptophan is found in:

>   lean meat, fish, chicken, turkey
>   cottage cheese
>   avocados
>   bananas
>   wheat germ

Alternatively, you could supplement 5-Hydroxytryptophan (5-HTP) – take according to directions.

6. Top Up Your Vitamins

If you're low in the essential B vitamins – including folic acid, B2, B6 and B12 – this can result in abnormally high levels of homocysteine, the toxic protein found in the blood described in the previous section. Take magnesium and zinc in the evening to help relax and calm your body.

Sadly, many people don't realise that what they eat may have contributed to their mood – or that it could be something as simple as food that corrects the problem.

Think about seaweed for a moment. It is a powerful source of iodine – the main support ingredient for thyroid and adrenal function. And yet, most people turn up their noses at the thought of eating it. Why? Because they don't like it. Why? Perhaps because they've been encouraged not to like it.

Marketing plays a huge role in determining what people like to eat. If the same energy and resources were poured into the marketing of seaweed as is done for fast-food burgers, people would love seaweed. Sadly, though, it is under-marketed, and worse, it is associated with 'unconventional' people and their food choices – hippies, and the like. History is filled with such propaganda: food is based more on social perception than on its genuine nutritive value, and large companies, and their investors, are interested in keeping it this way.

7. Get Your Hormones Checked By a Specialist Practitioner (Endocrinologist)

You don't have to be older for these to be imbalanced. Many changes can occur from as young as 35, and they have a profound effect on how you feel. The main hormones to get checked are testosterone, progesterone, oestrogen and insulin. Also run checks on thyroid, DHEA, liver and adrenals (especially cortisol).

8. Exercise. By Now, This Should Go Without Saying

Without question, imbalances in eating, poor sleep, physical illness, mood-altering drugs and exercise (or the lack of it) all have an impact on how you charge into your day. Problems in our physical well-being can affect how we think and feel, our mood and our ability to concentrate.

Take charge! Your physique is just too important to put issues such as these down to fate or age.

Summary: So to help beat depression and low mood, check off the following:

1. Avoid stimulants

2. Cut down hard on alcohol

3. Supplement with specific nutrients

4. Eat high-quality protein

5. Lift heavy weights

6. Get your hormones checked and balanced

13.
HOW TO AVOID
THE 3 CORPORATE CAREER
KILLERS – BURN-OUT,
BALE-OUT OR BOOTED OUT!

It will come as no surprise to most of us that our high-flying lifestyles, while often being held up as some ideal utopia of convenience and leisure, are, in fact, causing us to become more pressured by the day, compromising our professional performance, and accelerating us to an early grave.

Yes, we're talking about stress, which in the traditional sense is simply a physiological response to a perceived circumstance. If we feel threatened, pressured or even excited or exhilarated, certain physical reactions take place that nature designed to help us deal with the situation. In every case the response is geared to take place at a physical level – the Fight, Flight or Freeze response. In other words, deal with it, run away, or stay extremely still and hope you don't get noticed.

Once again, this goes way back to our hunter-gatherer days when our very survival depended on our ability to respond physically – whether hunting for food or fighting off predators or fellow humans. Our genetic profile hasn't changed since, and our adrenaline reactions today are exactly the same as they always have been.

> *We are hunter-gatherers in a corporate jungle.*

A key term in the definition of stress is *perceived* circumstance. Each person feels stress at different levels in different situations. For example, some people become stressed when they are running late for an appointment, while others couldn't care. Some people become extremely agitated when in a crowd of people, while others revel in that particular situation. Some enjoy the opportunity to speak in public, while others would rather jump out of a plane.

The level of stress we feel is determined by the perceived level of threat or challenge to ourselves, and it is a very individual response.

There are also some situations where we require stress to ensure we complete a certain task or challenge. A classic example would be an athlete competing at a high level. The stress and pressure on the body and mind are enormous, but they are also *required* to deliver the ability to perform at a maximal level. In many cases it's a good thing to invite the right type of stress into our lives in order to complete such an activity.

Sometimes the pressure of time, the prospect of failure or the demand of performance are necessary tools to enable us to do what we want to do – to achieve what we want to achieve.

In any event there is a 4-step process by which we usually make decisions, sometimes called the Stress Loop:

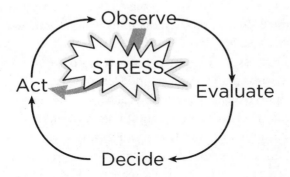

When under stress, it is often a matter of discipline and training that enables us to maintain clear and successful decision-making. Otherwise what tends to happen is we miss the middle two elements in the process and our responses to the situation become reactive, instinctive and sometimes without reason.

So let's have a quick look at what happens when we get stressed. First, the adrenal glands located on top of your kidneys inject varying amounts of epinephrine and norepinephrine, as well as the stress hormone cortisol. When combined these have the effect of:

» speeding up the heart rate
» increasing the bore and stroke of the heart's beating action
» increasing vasodilation of blood vessels supplying blood, oxygen and energy to the muscles and major organs of the body
» shutting down peripheral circulation to reserve blood pressure and supply for vital core areas of the body, and to reduce risk of blood loss in case of trauma injury to the limbs or surface areas
» increasing supply of sugars and fats into the bloodstream to ensure adequate energy supplies for fight or flight
» dilating pupils to increase peripheral vision
» increasing motor-neuron activity and speed for faster reactions and movements
» speeding up awareness and reaction times – often experienced during incidences of trauma, such as a traffic accident, where people are able to recall the event with extraordinary detail, and state that it felt as if it has happened 'in slow motion'

In situations where a physical action is appropriate ('acute' stress), these responses are fantastic. We become able to function at a far superior level than normal. But the modern dilemma is that for most of our lives we are almost entirely sedentary.

Most of the stress we encounter today tends to be faced from an office chair – and the stress never seems to end ('chronic' stress). There is no real resolution, and no realistic way of physically responding to the threat.

In the modern office it isn't appropriate to leap across the desk and strangle a colleague or your boss, and running away simply isn't an option either. In many cases – such as time pressure, decision-making or workload – it's a threat we can't even see.

The very responses that were programmed into us since the dawn of time to ensure our survival in a crisis, now become the greatest threat to our lives themselves:

» Heart rate and blood pressure increase, putting strain on our heart, blood vessels and arteries, placing us at greater risk of a heart attack, aneurism or stroke.
» Digestion suffers as the body prioritises activity to the muscles and major organs.
» Additional sugars and fats originally dumped into the bloodstream to use as extra energy are recycled and deposited

as dangerous visceral (central organ) fat, thanks to the after-effects of cortisol.

» The constant unresolved stress overloads the adrenal glands and pancreas – further compounded by the addition of coffee, cigarettes or other stimulant drugs – and these eventually malfunction, leading to adrenal fatigue or diabetes.

» You can't maintain a fast heartbeat and high blood pressure and also suppress your non-emergency bodily functions for long without running into trouble.

» There are other effects that may be less obvious. Adrenaline and cortisol both suppress the immune system, and long-term stress results in an increased susceptibility to bugs, infections, viruses and low-grade illnesses.

» The association between poor diet, chronic stress and cancer may also come about in this way, since the immune system helps to detect and eliminate early cancers.

» Chronic stress may also cause symptoms such as diarrhoea or constipation, tension headaches, backache, body aches and pains, fatigue, mood swings, irritation, impotence, sleep disorders and even depression.

Without the natural physical responses and nutritional resources available to us we become completely wired, yet worn out; exhilarated, yet exhausted; fired up, but fed up; and we can be assured of one thing – it will kill us sooner, rather than later.

> *'A hospital bed is a parked taxi with the meter running...' –*
> *Groucho Marx*

7 Things You Can Do to Avoid Boiling Over

1. Take a Deep Five whenever you feel wound up. That's five really deep breaths, filling the lungs with air from the diaphragm up, and exhaling completely. This action stimulates the vagus nerve, which connects the brain, heart and stomach. When the vagus nerve is activated in this manner, it has the immediate effect of slowing the heart rate, relaxing and calming the

stomach and digestion, and sending calming biofeedback signals up to the brain. The brain, in turn, instructs the body to reduce secretion of adrenaline, relax the 'fight or flight' muscles, and release your grip around the throat of whosoever was causing you the stress in the first place. As you perform your five deep breaths, concentrate on the sound, timing and movement of your breathing. This will help disconnect your thoughts from your immediate environment and the situation that may have been stressing you out.

2. Drink a glass of water or cup of camomile tea. It will slow you down for a minute, normalise blood viscosity (helping reduce blood pressure and cool the brain), and encourage your body to flush out toxins. Camomile tea also has a relaxing and calming effect, so is good as an evening drink taken a couple of hours before bed.

3. Eat something nutritious (an NDF). This will supply your body with important vitamins, nutrients, minerals and enzymes that will help counter the inflammatory and oxidative effects of stress. It will also help stave off hunger and the temptation to respond to pressure by eating fast, sugary snacks.

4. Do 20 deep squats, 20 press-ups, run the stairs, or get to the gym for a workout. This will relieve tension in the muscles, pump up your lymph system, oxygenate your blood, and provide a physical outlet to the effect of stress hormones.

5. To relieve tightness in the shoulders and help prevent tension headaches, do the three neck stretches: Tip, Tilt & Turn. Tip your head straight up, jutting the chin forwards. Tilt your head slowly to the left, then the right (like you see wrestlers do), feeling a stretch down the outside of the neck. Turn your head smoothly to look over your left, then right, shoulder.

6. Take up yoga. According to a recent article in *International Review of Psychiatry* (Volume 28, Issue 3, 2016), a number of benefits were identified from practising yoga, with management of stress, anxiety and other mental health conditions coming out strongly. The stretching, breathing and meditative effects of yoga continued to have lasting beneficial effects.

7. Shut down your email and turn off your smartphone. It stands to reason that business leaders who are expected to stay 'plugged in' – even after normal business hours – are more likely to experience greater levels of stress. (Even if you're not

actively looking at your emails, just being reachable is enough to significantly elevate cortisol levels.) Even when you're 'on the clock', checking emails can impede your ability to concentrate on more important matters at hand. How do you mitigate against the demands of a high-flying role? Cognitive Psychologist Paul Atchley recommends being disciplined about your use of mobile media and devices, and spending more time in nature.

8. Walking in bare feet in direct connection with the earth (as opposed to concrete or asphalt) is said to aid in 'grounding' by discharging built-up kinetic energy in your body. At a mechanical level, barefoot walking and running are wonderful methods to activate and strengthen all the bones and ligaments in your feet, improving balance, circulation and motor skills.

Is yoga useful as an exercise?

Yes. It will help you get a greater awareness of your body and the mind–muscle connections. Yoga is great for all the systems of the body and especially those old injuries, which cause imbalances in the muscle structures. Yoga can improve strength, suppleness, co-ordination, balance, digestion, breathing and focus. A bonus: according to research, the breathing, flexibility and pelvic-strengthening techniques of yoga assist many men and women to improve their bedroom skills!

14.
CIRCADIAN RHYTHMS

You go to bed, knowing that you need a good night's sleep to feel your best tomorrow. However, this isn't how it pans out. Hours later, you are lying wide awake, mind going at a hundred miles an hour, and you are so frustrated that even your partner's breathing sounds like a force nine gale. You finally drift off, only to find the alarm goes off five minutes later. Your workday begins – and you feel more tired than when you went to bed!

This is not normal, but sadly it is a recurring scenario affecting more and more businessmen and women on a nightly basis, especially those hard-charging high-fliers who tend to burn the candle at both ends. Quality sleep is critical to your health. It is a vital opportunity for defragging your mind, and for repair and maintenance of your body, your brain and your intellect.

We are only ever as healthy as our cells, and almost all cellular repair and maintenance takes place during sleep. It's the same as your car: in order for the mechanic to maintain and repair it, you need to park it up and switch it off.

A good night's sleep improves memory and mood, and keeps your cognition sharp along with offering better immune function, hormone balance and emotional resilience!

Getting to bed too late, or achieving less than six hours sleep a night, can actually do us harm. For brain health alone, this has the same effect as being hung-over. Aim to get to bed by 10.30 p.m. most nights. For the highest quality of sleep, it's best to be fatigued both mentally and physically, so challenge yourself in the gym everyday – and work out like you mean it!

Let's take an inside peek behind the scenes in a typical day for the busy business leader...

How much sleep do we need?

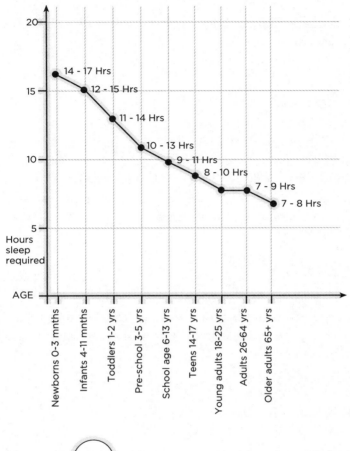

6.00-7.00 a.m.

You start waking up to the day. Your body temperature rises and a cocktail of hormones goes to work around your body. Glucose is released into the blood for an energy boost. Fertility is at its highest and a surge of growth hormone and testosterone means libido hits its peak at this time. It is also a great time for a workout or track session.

7.00-9.00 a.m.

As you get up and about, blood pressure and heart rate increase. The digestive system wakes up, and it's time for a good breakfast. Try porridge oats, a super smoothie or a boiled egg on sprouted-grain toast. (Sprouted-grain bread is made from wheat kernels that have been sprouted, ground and baked into bread; this process retains more of the nutrients with less gluten.) Your metabolism is most active now, so don't skip on breakfast.

9.00–12.00 noon

With hormone and concentration levels high, this is the best time to focus on difficult tasks. Apparently the optimum time to concentrate is in the morning, when you have been up for at least an hour. Your alertness peaks during the next 3–4 hours. Your body temperature is high, helping you to perform better, and fatigue hasn't set in yet.

12.00–2.00 p.m.

Stop for lunch. Some fresh air will also ease the post-lunch slump, so nip out for a walk, get some vitamin D on your skin and take the stairs on the way back to your desk.

2.00–4.00 p.m.

The body's efforts to digest lunch can mean a dip in energy if you have had too many simple or processed carbs. Drinking peppermint tea will help to aid digestion. Interestingly, it's also a good time to visit the dentist. Our pain threshold is highest now with peaking levels of endorphins, the body's natural painkillers.

4.00–6.00 p.m.

4 p.m. is a good time to have your late afternoon mini-meal. It's also a great time to jog. But not both. You're nicely warmed up, body temperature is at its highest and adrenaline is pumping. We reach our physical best now and it is no coincidence that most Olympic records have been set at this time.

6.00–8.00 p.m.

Time to dine. Try to eat about four hours before bedtime, to give your system time to digest the food. It's a good time to take a multi-vitamin because the body does most of its repair and maintenance work at night. Taking supplements with meals maximises nutrient absorption. It's also better to take minerals such as calcium, zinc and magnesium in the evening because they have a relaxing effect on the muscles and other tissue.

9.00–10.00 p.m.

By now your body temperature is falling, and rising levels of melatonin make us sleepy. Taking a relaxing warm bath will also speed this process. Good sleep patterns need regular bedtime rituals – we do it for our children and, as adults, our requirements are only fractionally different.

10.00 p.m.–3.00 a.m.

Body temperature falls as we enter deep sleep. Rising levels of the hormone vasopressin, which reduces urine output from the kidneys, mean you shouldn't need to go to the lavatory in the night. Inflammatory compounds called leukotrienes are at their highest. Taking vitamin C before bed calms cortisol and will help support and restore the adrenal glands. If you have a busy mind, you could also supplement with 5-HTP (5-Hydroxytryptophan), which calms brain and metabolic activity.

4.00–5.00 a.m.

You're least alert, and this may explain why many major accidents, such as at Chernobyl and Bhopal, have happened at this time. Body temperature and blood pressure reach their lowest point. Meanwhile, the pineal gland continues to secrete melatonin to make us extremely sleepy. Growth hormones secreted throughout the night are also busy repairing tissue and strengthening your bones, so the last thing your body wants is to wake up.

It is incredible that all this is done on the food you fed yourself with yesterday. This is why it's just as vital to look after your internal maintenance systems as your external appearance.

The Sleeping Brain

As you may already know, your brain continually oscillates between a variety of brain wave patterns, depending on the amount and type of activity we demand of it.

During the working day we vary between beta (quite active) and gamma (very active) wave patterns, depending on whether we're passively listening or absorbing information, or actively engaged in solving a problem or making a presentation.

When we sleep, however, we drop down through a much slower wave pattern called alpha waves, or REM (rapid eye movement) sleep. This is the brain state in which we dream. Our minds and imagination are still engaged, but our physical motor nerves are switched off.

Continuing to slow down brain activity, we pass through a phase of light sleep (theta waves) until we reach a state of deep sleep – almost comatose (delta waves). While in this state of deep, dreamless sleeping, our brain and other body structures are able to go through their optimal repair and maintenance processes, and it's the time of night when we get the best rest and restoration.

These sleep cycles repeat themselves throughout the night, so you end up going through REM sleep, light sleep and deep sleep over and over. Each cycle lasts for around 90 minutes, but what is less widely known is that within each cycle the percentage of deep sleep is progressively reduced, so your best ever sleep in terms of rest and recovery is always going to be that first two or three cycles, or the first four hours of sleep.

It's a bit like a series of trains passing through a station, and the timetable for those trains is based on the circadian rhythms linked to your 'home' geographical time zone.

If you miss the first cycle by staying up too late, you've missed that train and have to wait for the next, shorter train coming along behind it.

That's why we say in order to get the best *quality* of sleep, you need to get to bed by 10.30 p.m. – it's the best shot you have at restoring your energy, intelligence and drive.

Wealthy Body Wisdom: For a better night's sleep, include as many of the following in your evening routine.

» *Switch off after dinner. Turn off your smartphone and your emails. Have a conversation, read a book, listen to relaxing music, watch a comedy show.*

» *Before you go to sleep, or if you wake up later and can't sleep, always write your dominant thoughts down on paper and get them out of your mind.*

» *If crossing time zones, take exercise 1 hour before bed.*

» *Take a hot bath 30 minutes before bedtime with either calming fragrances (lavender, vanilla, sandalwood) or Epsom salts – the magnesium in the salts relaxes muscle and helps reduce cramps. Use the bath to relax and let go of your daily stress. When your body temperature is raised during a normal active day, it will naturally fall in the evening when you're less active, along with the ambient temperature outside. This drop in temperature helps initiate slumber, so having a hot bath before bed accelerates this process.*

» *Turn all lights off. Make your room as close to pitch black as possible. Light signals your brain that it's time to wake up.*

» *Check your bedroom for electro-magnetic fields (EMFs). These can disrupt the pineal gland and the production of melatonin and serotonin, and may have other negative effects as well. Don't have your cordless phone in your bedroom, switch your mobile to flight mode, and turn your WiFi off at the wall at night.*

» *Something warm, like a hot water bottle, may help soothe your anxieties, especially when*

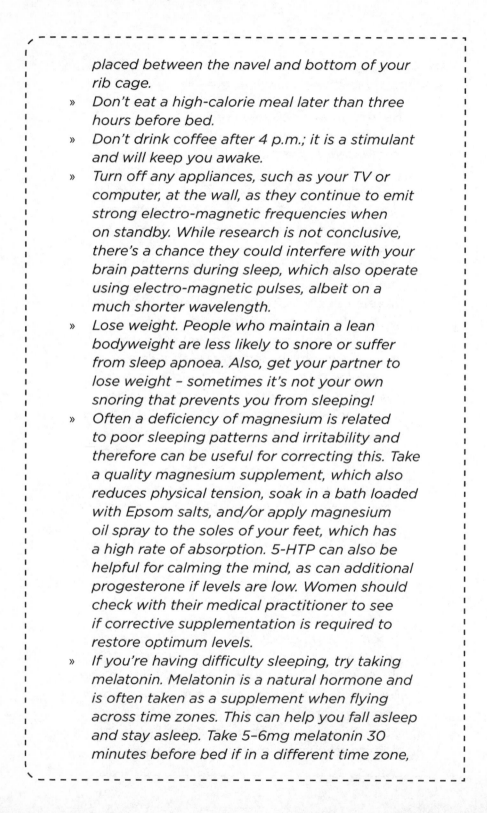

placed between the navel and bottom of your rib cage.

» Don't eat a high-calorie meal later than three hours before bed.

» Don't drink coffee after 4 p.m.; it is a stimulant and will keep you awake.

» Turn off any appliances, such as your TV or computer, at the wall, as they continue to emit strong electro-magnetic frequencies when on standby. While research is not conclusive, there's a chance they could interfere with your brain patterns during sleep, which also operate using electro-magnetic pulses, albeit on a much shorter wavelength.

» Lose weight. People who maintain a lean bodyweight are less likely to snore or suffer from sleep apnoea. Also, get your partner to lose weight – sometimes it's not your own snoring that prevents you from sleeping!

» Often a deficiency of magnesium is related to poor sleeping patterns and irritability and therefore can be useful for correcting this. Take a quality magnesium supplement, which also reduces physical tension, soak in a bath loaded with Epsom salts, and/or apply magnesium oil spray to the soles of your feet, which has a high rate of absorption. 5-HTP can also be helpful for calming the mind, as can additional progesterone if levels are low. Women should check with their medical practitioner to see if corrective supplementation is required to restore optimum levels.

» If you're having difficulty sleeping, try taking melatonin. Melatonin is a natural hormone and is often taken as a supplement when flying across time zones. This can help you fall asleep and stay asleep. Take 5–6mg melatonin 30 minutes before bed if in a different time zone, *or 3mg if in your home geography. For more tips and advice on sleep and international travel, please see below.*

» *Get to bed as early as possible. Your body (particularly your adrenal system) does a majority of its recharging between the hours of 10.30 p.m. and 1.00 a.m.*

» *You should go to bed and wake up at the same time each day, even on the weekends. This will help your body to get into a sleep rhythm and make it easier to fall asleep and get up in the morning.*

» *Don't drink any fluids within two hours of going to bed. This will reduce the likelihood of needing to get up and go to the bathroom.*

» *Avoid alcohol in the evening. This will raise your blood sugar initially, but when blood sugar drops too low you will wake up and find it difficult to go back to sleep. In this way, alcohol tends to have a second 'kick'.*

» *If sleep disruption is constant, you wake up more tired than you went to bed, or your energy crashes during the day without reason, have your hormones checked by a specialist anti-ageing doctor or endocrinologist. You may be suffering from adrenal fatigue (see page 107).*

International Travel Tips

As international speakers we fly at least once a month and these are usually long-haul flights, so we have some tricks and tips to prevent illness and time zone disruption.

» Have a regular exercise programme in place before you leave. This helps keep your joints, ligaments and capillaries flexible.

A fitter circulatory system will have a better blood flow and enhanced capillary function during the long hours of sitting.

» Walk around frequently when on the plane to prevent the risk of pulmonary embolism.

» Get a good night's sleep before you leave, or take a night flight where possible.

» Get enough sun exposure in order to optimise your vitamin D levels before you leave. This will help you adapt to your destination time zone and boost your immune system. Take oral vitamin D in the morning of your new destination and melatonin in the evening to help your circadian rhythms sync in with that time zone. According to recent research, adults need about 8,000 IUs of oral vitamin D3 per day.

» Astaxanthin is another powerful natural antioxidant to add to your supplement arsenal – found to help protect from radiation exposure related to flying and airport X-ray scanners. Take 4mg per day leading up to your flight and during your time away.

» Avoid eating processed and high-sugar foods and drinks before or during your flight (well any time actually!). Instead eat plenty of whole foods and drink water – one glass of water for every hour of flight is a good guide.

» Pack some healthy back-up snacks just in case you get caught on a 'peanuts only' flight. Get stuck on one of these and you are sure to grab the first bite of pizza, fries or cheeseburger you can get your hands on the minute you're off the plane. Having back-up snacks helps you stick to your healthy habits and prevents mental fatigue and lethargy. We always pack vitamin C, seed, berry and nut mix, super greens and organic health/protein bars. Hard-boiled eggs, cheese, carrots, cucumbers and celery stalks filled with nut butter or goat cheese are examples of snack foods that can also carry you over to when you reach your destination if healthier foods may not be available.

» Wash your hands regularly and avoid touching your mouth, nose or eyes. Whether you are on a plane or in the airport you can transfer germs from a contaminated surface into your body. Use hand wipes if you're not near a hand-washing facility.

» Your first line of defence against travel bugs is a strong immune system. Many people can be exposed or infected with a germ but it doesn't mean it will make them ill. It all depends on the ground work you have put into your health and immunity.

» Have a high-quality probiotic (good bacteria) in your travel bag. Eat plenty of fermented foods like kefir, natto and sauerkraut, which are natural sources of probiotics. These improve and strengthen digestion and help prevent the constipation that many people get while travelling.

» Don't forget a quick clean-up of your hotel room when you check in. A quick whip around with antiseptic wet wipes on taps, handles and countertops, washing glasses, and crucially the TV remote can reduce your risk of exposure to pathogens.

» When travelling don't suffer quietly unhealthy food offerings put before you. Speak up to the servers at the restaurants and ask questions! Is there a greater range of fresh vegetables available? I only eat free-range grass-fed beef. Do you carry free-range organic chicken?

15.
RESILIENCE

So what comes first – good mental health or good physical health?

There is a flaw in the way we think about disease; we treat symptoms rather than the root cause. We treat parts rather than the whole.

The body is an extremely complex system and it needs the base components kept in tip-top condition first. This means:

»   lots of movement
»   the right nutrients
»   good sleep habits
»   a non-toxic environment
»   balanced and optimised hormones
»   meaning and purpose
»   social connection

All these elements affect the business mind, mood and motivation, the results of which then spiral out to affect our whole body. Ours is a system of biofeedback, and the brain is the most chemically sensitive area in the body. Its operations require 20 per cent of the entire body's blood flow, and it contains 640km (400 miles) of blood vessels.

It is now well documented that many people consume up to 225g (8oz) of sugar a day, much of it hidden in processed food and drink. Sugar raises cortisol and adrenaline levels during the non-stress times when we don't need them.

If you don't get enough sleep, your body has difficulty getting your master hormones regulated.

If you are exposed to environmental toxins, these are an added burden on your biology.

Next, if your gut flora has been knocked out with antibiotics and processed foods, this leads to further emotional and psychological disturbances.

Hormones – Drive-train of the Corporate Physique

Your hormones are the master controllers of your physique, quietly keeping everything running optimally and organised within your body. But when they get knocked out of balance they cause mayhem and chaos, beginning with your brain.

For most women this is not news, as information about female hormonal issues is widely available, but more men than ever before are now presenting with higher than normal oestrogen levels, and this is leading to an epidemic of male 'gender-morphing'.

Today, the average man has a testosterone level that is lower than it was 50 years ago by 15–50 per cent (depending on the study you read). His fertility is lower than ever, and there has been a 300 per cent rise in breast-reduction surgery (mastectomies) for men in the last 10 years.

Oestrogen dominance is also thought to be responsible for many types of cancers experienced by both genders, especially as our environment and state of health changes.

The problem?

Causes of hormone imbalances are many and varied, and may include a combination of factors.

Drugs

Pharmaceutical hormones, such as those used in hormone-replacement therapy or birth control pills, can increase oestrogen. Now, whether we take them actively or absorb them from drinking water, we are nonetheless immersed in a plethora of harmful oestrogens, and researchers are only beginning to understand the extent of this exposure on our health.

Meat

The meat from intensively farmed animals frequently contains a cocktail of man-made oestrogens found in most herbicides, insecticides and pesticides. 'Battery' cattle and poultry also harbour residue from antibiotics, growth hormone and other veterinary drugs that have been mixed into the feed they eat. In addition, soy-based feeds, that many animals are raised on, are high in oestrogens. These oestrogenic compounds are stored in their fat and muscle fibres and are also passed into the milk we drink. Be sure to eat only meat raised on organic, free-range pastures, and not grain- or soy-fed animals.

Pesticides and Insecticides

Eat only organic, pesticide-free and chemical-free fruits and vegetables, if possible. Be aware that atrazine and dieldrin are endocrine-disrupting chemicals (EDCs) that can still be present in non-organic produce, and many agricultural pesticides and insecticides work by 'sterilising' the insects with high doses of oestrogen, in the same way the human contraceptive pill works. In June 2011 the *International Journal of Environmental Research and Public Health* published a paper explaining this process, highlighting links between exposure to endocrine-disruptor pesticides and breast and prostate cancer, and reproductive and sexual development anomalies in humans. It also cited studies demonstrating residues of these chemicals in fruits and vegetables in excess of the Acceptable Daily Intake (ADI) and Acute Reference Dose guidelines.[23]

'Fake' Foods

This means that most foods that come out of a box, bag or can should be off your list. Basically, if a caveman couldn't eat it, you shouldn't eat it. Most of the chemicals used in these highly processed foods cause disruption to your hormones. The linings of most plastic containers and cans also contain Bisphenol-A (BPA) – another pseudo-oestrogen, hormone-disrupting chemical.

Preservatives

Parabens are considered xenoestrogens, which means they can act as a pseudo-oestrogen, or oestrogen mimic. Parabens are used in cosmetics as a preservative and are in just about everything you put on your skin, face and hair. Here are a few: moisturiser, lipstick, foundation, 'anti-wrinkle' creams, toothpaste, concealer, eye makeup, makeup removers, shampoo, sunscreen, bandages, topical ointments, deodorant and eye drops.

Parabens are also found in food products: mustard, processed vegetables, frozen dairy products, salad dressing, mayonnaise, jelly, soft drinks and baked goods, as well as many household or industrial products, including textiles and glues.

As the evidence rises against these chemicals there are many products now being made paraben-free. So become a label detective, and make the safer, healthier choice.

Plastics

Avoid eating and drinking out of plastic as much as possible as the xenoestrogens they contain are imposters that mimic your biological oestrogen. As mentioned above, this is most commonly a chemical called BPA, an insidious oestrogen that gets into your food from heated plastics. BPA is also released into your food when you microwave meals on plastic trays or in plastic bags, or if your plastic water bottles are allowed to get warm and you then drink the water. You might not drink warm water *per se*, but think of all of those thousands of bottles of water – before arriving at your supermarket, they often sit in crates, on docks, in hot countries, or in the back of uncooled trucks. That's where the warming can happen.

Always empty frozen foods into a saucepan, glass or ceramic bowl before heating or thawing. Also remove any cling film.

Never use cling film over foods – least of all hot foods. Instead, use wax paper or place in a glass container. This is particularly important for children and in school lunch boxes.

Keep water bottles in a cool, dry, dark place. It is best to drink water filtered with reverse osmosis filters.

Cosmetics and Soaps

Triclosan, another synthetic oestrogen, is present in antibacterial soaps. Triclosan has been known to disrupt hormones in bullfrogs – so clearly you should never feed soap to your bullfrog.

Wealthy Body Wisdom: *When the body is subjected to high levels of sustained, or chronic, stress, it 'steals' progesterone to manufacture the stress hormone cortisol, often leaving an excess of oestrogen.*

Eating unfermented soy products like tofu and soy milk may also raise your oestrogen levels, as they contain phytoestrogens. Fermented soy products like tempeh, miso, fermented soy beans and soy sauce are relatively oestrogen-free.

Correct Oestrogen Dominance and Regain Your Alpha Drive

Bacterial imbalance in the gut, and other problems that compromise digestion, interfere with the elimination of oestrogen from the body. An unhealthy digestive tract fuelled by refined carbohydrates, processed foods, gluten and alcohol can lead to 'leaky gut' and an up-regulation of an enzyme called B-glucouronidase. This breaks apart bound oestrogen that is getting excreted out of the body through the intestines, making it easier to reabsorb back into the body.

Include a twice-daily probiotic with 15 billion units, or eat more fermented foods like kefir, sauerkraut or tempeh, which are teeming with natural probiotic bacteria. For example, a 110g (40z) serving of fermented cabbage (sauerkraut – one of the easiest ones to make) contains over 10 trillion healthy bacteria – more than found in 100 probiotic capsules!

Beneficial bacteria can prevent oestrogen reabsorption by reducing dysbiosis, as it is high levels of bad bacteria that uncouple the bond between oestrogen and glucuronic acid.

Store probiotic supplements in the refrigerator and take them on an empty stomach.

Boost your best detox organ – the liver.

Synthetic oestrogens have a much stronger, stimulating effect when they are not cleared out quickly from the body. The liver breaks down oestrogen, so alcohol consumption, drug use, and other negative lifestyle habits that impair healthy liver function may increase oestrogen build-up.

Include plenty of insoluble fibre in your diet, as it binds to excess oestrogen and is excreted. It's also good for your gut bacteria. Good sources include oat bran; the skins of fruits and vegetables (apples, pears, berries, tomatoes, aubergines, courgettes and carrots); almonds; seeds; dried beans; and whole-grain foods.

Where possible, choose fresh organic products to reduce your exposure to hormone additives.

The body requires sufficient intake of zinc, magnesium, vitamin B6 and other essential nutrients, not only to break down and eliminate oestrogens but also to aid the function of enzymes responsible for the conversion of testosterone to oestrogen.

Clean up your sleep habits. Poor sleep causes a reduction in the hormone melatonin, which also helps protect against oestrogen dominance.

Eat more of the natural oestrogen-blocking foods. Cruciferous vegetables will help, and these should not just be a colourful garnish to your meal. *Eat them.* Broccoli, cauliflower, cabbage, kale and Brussels sprouts are all members of the *Brassica* family of vegetables, and contain a chemical called diindolylmethane, a compound that naturally binds to oestrogen and removes it from the body.

(Time and again when we review clients' food diaries, there are almost no coloured vegetables. We are also constantly amazed at the number of 'vegetarians' who also do not eat vegetables!)

Citrus fruits; spices such as turmeric and herbs such as fenugreek; supplements such as chlorella and passionflower (which contains chrysin), as well as resveratrol capsules – all help to reduce excess oestrogens by blocking the enzyme aromatase, which converts androstenedione and testosterone into oestrogen in men, contributing to the formation of 'man-boobs'.

Oestrogen dominance in both men and women has become a real health concern. It's important for us to become aware that the foods, and the food products we use, are not just contributing to the aesthetic problems of being overweight but can have far-reaching consequences for our health. Hormone awareness is not just for women: if you are experiencing symptoms of oestrogen dominance or testosterone deficiency, please see a specialist doctor or endocrinologist for complete hormone testing.

Common symptoms for men include, but aren't limited to:

» Diminished sexual desire and interest, and reduced erectile function and ejaculatory quality

» Changes in mood with decreases in intellectual activity and spatial-orientation ability, fatigue, depression, irritability, and loss of drive and focus
» Decrease in lean body mass with associated diminution of muscle volume and strength
» Loose and saggy skin
» Decrease in bodily hair and skin thickness and quality
» Decreased bone density, leading to osteoporosis
» Excessive gas and bloating
» Increased body fat, especially in the abdominal area

Common symptoms for women include, but aren't limited to:

» Breast cancer
» Cold hands and feet as a symptom of thyroid dysfunction
» Decreased sex drive
» Depression with anxiety or agitation
» Dry eyes
» Endometrial (uterine) cancer
» Fat gain, especially around the abdomen, hips and thighs
» Fatigue
» Fibrocystic breasts
» Hair loss
» Headaches
» Infertility
» Irregular menstrual periods
» Irritability
» Insomnia
» Memory loss
» Mood swings
» Polycystic ovaries
» Sluggish metabolism
» Thyroid dysfunction mimicking hypothyroidism
» Uterine cancer
» Uterine fibroids

Want to enjoy a healthy and vital business life with all your marbles intact? Observe what almost everyone else is doing – and do the opposite.

Wealthy Body Wisdom: *Physical health is the cornerstone of executive strength, energy and performance.*

16.
CORPORATE CANCER

Cancerous cells are always being created in the body. It's an on-going process that has existed for aeons. Consequently, there are parts of your immune system designed to seek out and destroy cancer cells.

Cancer has been around as long as mankind, but only in the twentieth century did the number of cancer cases explode.[24] Contributing to this increase are the excessive amounts of toxins and pollutants, electromagnetic stress; high-stress lifestyles that zap the immune system; and poor-quality, highly processed junk food that may be full of pesticides or which has been irradiated or made from genetically modified ingredients. None of these factors existed even 200 years ago.

All these elements weaken the immune system, and alter the internal environment in the body to promote the growth of cancer.

Generally cancer is not a mysterious disease that suddenly attacks you out of the blue, something that you can't do anything about. It has definite causes that you can correct if your body has enough time, and if you take action to change the internal environment to one that creates health while at the same time attacking cancerous cells and tumours by exploiting their weaknesses.

Cancer tumours begin when more cancerous cells are being created than your overworked, depleted immune system can destroy.

Constant exposure to tens of thousands of man-made chemicals from birth onwards can lead to the creation of too many free radicals and excessive numbers of cancerous cells.

Combined with an immune system weakened from a diet of refined and over-processed food, the immune system at some point is no longer able to keep cancer in check, which starts to grow in your body.

With an immune system that is not capable of destroying the excessive numbers of cancerous cells that develop, these will sooner or later survive and multiply. And then you have the beginnings of cancer.

And, of course, our diets, devoid of vital antioxidants and loaded with sugar, refined carbohydrates and alcohol don't help. Refined carbohydrates digest so fast they act like sugar, and cancer cells love sugar. They have about 15 times more receptor cells for capturing sugar than healthy cells do.

Helping overcome cancer is a process of reversing the conditions that allowed the cancer to develop.

The more support you give your body, the better you will be at handling any possible side effects of chemotherapy and radiation therapy, and the better your body's immune cells will be at fighting cancer.

A baseline approach to cancer is centred on making your body healthier. In other words, building 'host resistance'.

If I think back to my attempts at vegetable gardening, I know it is the soil that determines which plants will grow and flourish and which will fall to disease and pest attack – and it's exactly the same in our bodies.

If our inner 'soil' is acidic, stressed, flooded with toxic chemicals, and depleted of nutrients and sleep, cancer can, and will, make its home there.

Cancer will not always be defeated by heavy drugs and scalpels because, ultimately, it is the state of your immune system that determines whether or not you get sick.

Also, be aware that if you have had cancer treated successfully – it is just that cancer that has been 'fixed'. In many cases something caused the cancer to proliferate in the first place – especially in adults – and unless you take significant steps to change that, it will surely return.

It is *not* a game of roulette, as we incorrectly assume or have been told; prevention is the best antidote to boosting your immune system into a 'lean, mean, disease-fighting machine'.

So pay attention to your lifestyle habits, nutritional density, alkalinity, exercise and sleep, learn how to relieve stress and optimise your hormones and exposure to sunlight.

Wealthy Body Action Points: *21 ways to hedge your bets against cancer...*

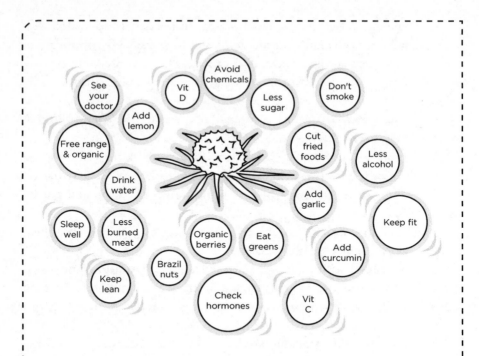

Follow as many of these as you can. That means all of them.

» *Avoid excess sugar. Cancer cells feed off glucose, which helps tumours grow faster and spread more rapidly throughout the body. Beware of hidden sugars in bread, salad dressings, cooking sauces and juice drinks.*

» *Switch from French fries and crisps to mashed or baked sweet potatoes. A potential cancer-causing compound called acrylamide forms as a result of the chemical changes that occur in foods when they're commercially fried or roasted.*

» *Reduce your intake of alcohol. When you drink, the alcohol in your body is converted into a toxic chemical called acetaldehyde. This can damage your DNA and stop your cells from repairing that damage, which can lead to cancer and liver damage, and can increase the* levels of hormones such as oestrogen. Wines are also laced with traces of agrochemicals, unless organic, which contribute to the toxic load on your body. (Remember that 15 out of every 100 cases of breast cancer are caused directly by alcohol.[25])

» Add garlic to everything you can. The sulphur in garlic has been shown to boost the immune system's response to cancer and even reduce tumour growth.

» Curcumin, from turmeric, is another food that has strong anti-inflammatory properties and shows great promise in the fight against cancer. Initial research suggests curcumin can suppress tumour initiation, and reduce the spread of cancer to other parts of the body. It also has neural benefits, and may be influential in preventing Alzheimer's disease, Parkinson's disease and stroke. Curries containing curcumin are also beneficial to the circulatory system – and that may just add some spice to your love life!

» Of course, always finish eating your broccoli, greens and brightly coloured vegetables for their powerful antioxidant effects. They should represent at least half the content of your plate.

» Mix organic blueberries with your morning smoothie, a powerful source of antioxidants and polyphenols that prevent cell damage in the body.

» Drink green tea, which contains antioxidants, instead of coffee.

» Sprinkle crushed Brazil nuts over your salad. Brazils are high in selenium, a mineral deficient in most of our soils.

» Don't eat too much charred meat. Grilling meat can create a variety of cancer-causing

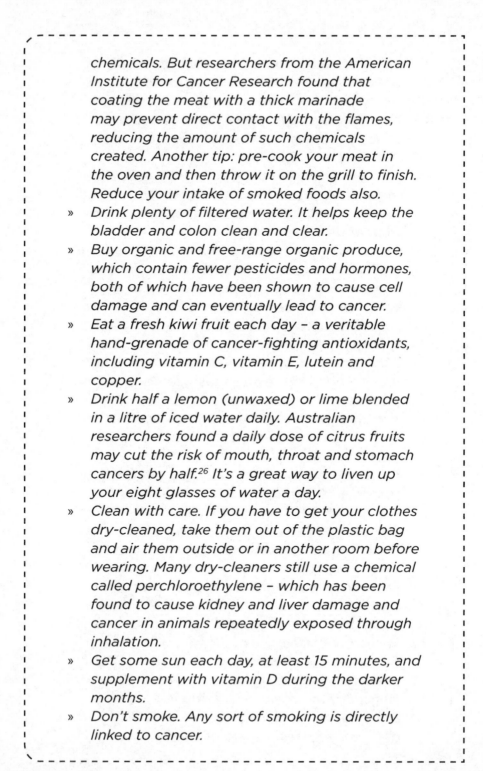

chemicals. But researchers from the American Institute for Cancer Research found that coating the meat with a thick marinade may prevent direct contact with the flames, reducing the amount of such chemicals created. Another tip: pre-cook your meat in the oven and then throw it on the grill to finish. Reduce your intake of smoked foods also.

» Drink plenty of filtered water. It helps keep the bladder and colon clean and clear.

» Buy organic and free-range organic produce, which contain fewer pesticides and hormones, both of which have been shown to cause cell damage and can eventually lead to cancer.

» Eat a fresh kiwi fruit each day – a veritable hand-grenade of cancer-fighting antioxidants, including vitamin C, vitamin E, lutein and copper.

» Drink half a lemon (unwaxed) or lime blended in a litre of iced water daily. Australian researchers found a daily dose of citrus fruits may cut the risk of mouth, throat and stomach cancers by half.[26] It's a great way to liven up your eight glasses of water a day.

» Clean with care. If you have to get your clothes dry-cleaned, take them out of the plastic bag and air them outside or in another room before wearing. Many dry-cleaners still use a chemical called perchloroethylene – which has been found to cause kidney and liver damage and cancer in animals repeatedly exposed through inhalation.

» Get some sun each day, at least 15 minutes, and supplement with vitamin D during the darker months.

» Don't smoke. Any sort of smoking is directly linked to cancer.

» *Have regular check-ups. Early detection is vital. Men: once you're over the age of 40, get a prostate check every five years, and monitor your PSA levels (Prostate Specific Antigen) each time you get a medical.*

» *Keep lean and fit. As we gain weight, we not only have an increased risk of developing cancer, but we also decrease the chance of successfully fighting any possible tumours that may establish themselves.*

» *Get your hormones checked, balanced and optimised. The homeostasis of your entire body is orchestrated by your hormones and, when they fall out of balance, all the body's protective functions are compromised, and it may actually provide an environment that promotes the establishment and spread of some cancers.*

» *Supplement with liposomal vitamin C, which, it is claimed, has an absorption and cellular delivery rate comparable with intravenous (IV) administration. Liposomal vitamin C uses phospholipids to wrap around the vitamin C molecule and act as a carrier, thus allowing direct access through the walls of cells. You can purchase this online in the UK through Detox People (www.detoxpeople.eu), or at www.mercola.com. Vitamin C is a powerful antioxidant, which helps neutralise cell-damaging free radicals when taken orally. When used intravenously, the vitamin appears to also directly attack pathogens and has shown promise for treating a wide range of infectious diseases as well as burns and for boosting your immune system. Check with your doctor to see if this is available.*

17.
THERE'S NO NEED TO GET OLD

The conventional approach to ageing and healthcare is one in which we are encouraged to switch off and do nothing – just leave it up to the experts. It is difficult to make sensible choices and be in control when you are switched off or ill informed. This is nothing more than 'learned powerlessness', so now is your chance to wake up and understand what your body actually wants you to know: you do have control.

We have created three levels of personal interventions to drive your way through to an extended career and life expectancy. We call this process Climbing the Wealthy Body Ladder.

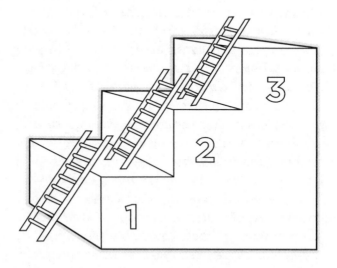

Level 1: Turn Back Your Age Clock

» Increase the number of your foot strikes each day. Add extra
exercise opportunities such as climbing stairs two at a time,
walking up the escalator and parking further away from the
shops.

» Drink clean filtered water regularly – it is the body's
lubrication. We lose half a litre of water every day just
through breathing. We naturally dehydrate with age. This
problem can be overcome by regularly drinking water
throughout the day *before* you feel thirsty.

» Keep a diary of how much you eat and drink for a week,
since 'eating amnesia' is endemic. This also helps you identify
problem eating patterns – for example, are you *really* eating
your 8–9 servings of coloured vegetables every day?

» To establish a stable metabolic and energy curve, eat 4–5
small nutrient-dense meals a day – especially if you are
training to maintain a strong, functional physique.

» Become a food detective. Start reading and understanding the
labels on all the foods you eat. So, if you wanted to reduce
your intake of sugar, look out for ingredients ending in '–ose'
(glucose, sucrose, fructose, maltose, dextrose) and for other
forms of sugar (corn syrup, high-fructose corn syrup, corn
starch, maize starch, fruit juice concentrate). Ideally these
should not appear on the label at all, and certainly not in the
first five ingredients!

» Find a picture of the physique you would most like to
resemble. Pin this on the ceiling above your bed. It is very
motivational and helps programme your subconscious. There
are no limits to where you can take your body shape.

» Always eat breakfast. Those who don't are fatter because they
are usually eating too much too late at night.

» Add variety and avoid eating the same foods daily. We are
continually amazed at how repetitive people's diets are, which
can also cause allergies and intolerances.

» Enjoy fresh fruit for snacks, but no more than 15 per cent of
your diet should come from eating fruit. It is *not* a substitute
for vegetables, and it is not an either/or option.

» Organic vegetables and fruits, organic lean proteins and fresh
clean water are the base requirements for fantastic ageing.

» Start looking out for, and avoiding, all foods with hydrogenated oils and (trans-) fats. They are powerful inflammatories, and promote cancer growth, as they readily oxidise. These often include items made with corn, safflower, sunflower, peanut and canola oils. Check the label, looking for 'Trans-Fats' in the nutritional breakdown.

» Instead include sources of healthy essential fats, such as avocado, coconut oil, organic pasture-fed butter, extra virgin olive oil, pasture-fed meats, raw dairy products, nuts and seeds. Cheap refined vegetable oils and ingredients containing trans-fats should be removed from your house and discarded.

» Cut your portion sizes down. Buy smaller dinner plates to help get things in the right perspective. Begin by cutting back your portion sizes by 10 per cent.

» In this beginning stage, and if you can't do without sweeteners, choose xylitol or stevia or take chromium supplements.

» Immediately cut back on alcohol. Alcohol inhibits your liver and kidney function and leads to an accumulation of oestrogens, accelerating weight gain and ill-health.

» Start the day with a glass of freshly blended lemon juice (we blend half a fresh lemon with 1 litre distilled water). Lemons have the most amazing properties when consumed fresh. Just like your digestive system, lemons are anionic – in other words, they are one of the only foods we eat which are totally charged with negative ions. This positions them as an alkaline pH element, thus providing balance and a massive boost to your digestive system. Most other foods we eat are cationic (positively charged). Lemons are also known to stimulate liver enzymes, are loaded with high-potency vitamin C, rich in potassium, and can help repair damaged skin cells from within the body. The liver is your main detox station, and replaces itself roughly every 90 days, so drink a glass of lemon detox juice every morning to give it a helping hand.

» Don't fill up on breads and grains as a dietary staple – especially at the expense of other, more nutritious foods. Don't be fooled by 'natural', 'brown', 'granary' or breads with just a few seeds sprinkled on top. These are marketing ploys designed to conjure up home-grown and wholesome emotions.

» Grains are used to fatten cattle, and they will fatten you too. You end up eating what your food has eaten. Aim to reduce the amount of grains in your diet – even by just a modest amount. You'll find it easier to lose weight, maintain high energy and strong immunity, and reduce inflammation. The only carbs you really need to eat are your vegetables.

» Be choosy. Organic fresh produce is best, but only if it comes from close to home and doesn't sit in your fridge for days. If this can't be achieved, then opt for frozen organic, as there is less time-lapse between harvesting and freezing and so fewer nutrients are lost.

» Don't eat beige-coloured processed foods (pastries, pasties, crumbed or fried) or empty white foods. These cause wear and tear on your DNA, damaging cellular function. When eating out, we are totally amazed by the food we see left behind on dinner plates. It is often the fried and crumbed foods that get eaten, and the coloured foods (salads and vegetables) that are, sadly, left behind.

» Avoid quick-release, processed and fast foods. They can cause inflammation, which disturbs the body's delicate internal balances. Your body is not designed to process these effectively.

» Supplement daily with a quality multi-vitamin/mineral, anti-oxidant and an omega-3. The nutrient content in your food varies widely.

» Stop drinking your calories. Unless freshly squeezed, most fruit drinks are just flavoured sugar water. Because the pasteurisation process necessary to enhance shelf life has destroyed most of the micronutrients, all that remains are sugar calories. Even 'freshly squeezed' juices are simply all the sugar calories extracted from the fruit, leaving behind the vital roughage and fibre that slow down absorption to a reasonable level, and the material you need to aid digestion and elimination. Instead of orange juice – eat a fresh orange. Instead of apple juice – eat a fresh apple. This isn't tricky.

» Cut out the S foods (stimulants). Eating foods too high in sugar, salt and caffeine will upset your blood sugar, making you crave more quick-fix foods and exacerbating mood swings. Stimulants have a tremendously ageing effect on your body by overtaxing your pituitary, adrenal and thyroid glands, leading to excessive fatigue, poor resilience and recovery, and breakdown.

» Be positive, and keep challenging yourself. Maintain a happy outlook on life.

Wealthy Body Wisdom: *Being in great shape is the best retirement plan.*

Level 2: Improve Your Life Position

» Concentrate on getting your foot strikes/footsteps up to 10,000 a day. Use a pedometer or pedometer app to keep track.

» Up the ante on vegetables now. Try to eat at least half to three-quarters of your vegetables raw. Important anti-ageing enzymes are destroyed by cooking. The added benefit of eating raw vegetables is chewing, as this burns more calories and improves the facial muscles – look on it as face fitness! You will also feel full quicker and it suppresses cravings. Raw is fantastic for a healthy waistline and skin. It also promotes healthy elimination by speeding up the movement of toxic material out of the body.

» Chew your food well. Chewing (mastication) is the mechanism installed by nature to break food down in our mouths from large chunks into a more easily digested paste. This makes it easier for your intestines to absorb nutrients from the food particles as they pass through, and therefore offer better supply and support to all your body's operational systems. In addition, when you chew your food thoroughly, your mouth releases a chemical called hypothiocyanate, a natural – and powerful – antibiotic that helps protect you from uploading various bugs and germs which may have attached themselves to your food. There are other obvious advantages to chewing your food more thoroughly. The longer you chew, the more time it will take you to finish a meal, and eating slowly may help you to eat less, thus avoiding the chances of weight gain. Of course, it's best to eat in a relaxed, non-distracted environment; eating on the run or while you're working – or watching TV – is not conducive to the proper breakdown, digestion or absorption of your food.

» Eating should be based around controlling insulin, selecting low glycaemic foods, and optimising the amount of nutrients you can.

» Now you've established a regular pattern of eating four small meals a day, you can up the ante by extending the period within which you *don't* eat. At this level we recommend not eating at least four hours before bed, and waiting until mid-morning if possible for your first meal of the day (breakfast). This is so you don't go to bed with any spare calories that might convert to fat storage overnight, and it allows the body to get on with the job of repair and maintenance, rather than the overload of digesting a meal. Additionally, your metabolic engine will seek fuel from stored fats first thing in the morning, instead of sourcing energy from an early breakfast (although remember to have your morning lemon detox juice regardless). Now, we realise this won't work in a number of situations (an early start before business meetings when travelling, for example), but if you *can* manage it, your body will gradually begin to increase the amount of fat it burns for fuel during the day. You'll still get to eat plenty of nutrient-dense foods from the likes of vegetables, nuts, seeds, eggs, healthy oils and fresh organic meats, but you'll be eating fewer processed and simple carbs if you've reached this level on the Wealthy Body Ladder, so overall calorie intake should remain about the same. We're just trying to switch the *source* of that fuel to your best advantage. Other advantages include:

» increases insulin and leptin sensitivity, reducing risk of chronic disease, including diabetes, heart disease and even cancer

» increases ghrelin levels – your hunger hormone, which helps reduce the urge to over-eat

» increases your ability to become 'fat-adapted'. In other words your ability to burn more fats from storage

» decreases inflammation, triglyceride levels, weight gain and risk of metabolic disease

» cleanses and 'defrags' the brain, through a process known as autophagy

» Keep regular healthy sleep patterns. Sleep is clean-up time for the body, and the key to feeling alert, focused and in good form. Lack of sleep decreases leptin, the hormone that regulates your appetite, making you crave sweets and carbohydrates during the day.

» If you can't do so already, learn to cook. This gives you control, understanding and knowledge over what is in your food.

» Don't buy foods with more than five ingredients, or any that have artificial flavourings and colourings. The compounding toxic mix of these in our finely tuned systems promotes ageing.

» Don't buy foods with contents or ingredients you cannot pronounce. Nature did not design us to eat them. Learn to discriminate between foods made in a kitchen and food products made in a lab.

» Get some sunshine; around 15–20 minutes of sunshine a day can dramatically improve vitamin D levels, which are important for good health. Take care not to over-expose your skin, however. In winter you may need to supplement with vitamin D if your blood profiles are low. Get them tested regularly so you know your exact numbers. This will help rectify any deficiency with greater accuracy.

» Eat mainly organic vegetables; they are a far superior food because they are grown in healthy, naturally farmed soils. Just like us, a plant can only reflect the food it feeds upon. As you will be living healthier and for longer, it's also a wise choice for the environment!

» Be constantly aware that low fluid, low vitamin, low mineral and low phytochemical intake from too few vegetables leads to low energy levels, and will leave you vulnerable to ill health and to disease. Vegetables are often considered unglamorous and simple, but they are one of the essential keys to losing weight, having wonderful skin, and turning back your age clock.

» To get that little extra high-quality nutrition, juicing or blended smoothies are excellent to rejuvenate your body (as long as they are not made mainly of fruit; we recommend one piece per serving).

» Up the resistance levels in your workouts by training with heavier weights. Only through progressive overload do we become stronger, fitter and more energised. Uniquely, lifting heavy weights is an effective tool for balancing hormones, managing depression and elevating resting metabolic rate.

» Avoid pollution, keep well away from cigarette smoke, heavy traffic and polluted environments.

» Drink from glass containers only (not plastic) and check your hydration levels by keeping your urine straw-coloured, no darker.

» Relax, chill out. Whether it is through meditation, yoga, or simply finding and pursuing your passion, do what works best for you to regularly reduce your stress levels. Don't worry about tomorrow – it hasn't happened yet – and yesterday is in the past and cannot be undone.

» Cut out tea and coffee, drink only herbal teas.

» Become an even better food detective, be assertive and know how to order effectively and strategically in restaurants. You are far more likely to eat a day's worth of worthless calories in just one meal if you are unaware of its contents.

» Choose only organic, free-range, pasture-fed lean meat. Up to 85 per cent of microorganisms are now depleted from our intensively farmed soils. In addition, there are higher levels of chemicals (herbicides, insecticides, pesticides, fungicides, growth hormones, antibiotics) entering this environment, as the animals require more veterinary products to stay alive. We are then eating this depleted and chemically tainted product. Free-range stock are naturally fitter and healthier animals, and enjoy a superior quality of life.

» Make it a priority to educate yourself and keep up to date with what is in your food and where it comes from. Set an agenda to subscribe to the articles, blogs and posts of independent research organisations and qualified individuals who operate in the field of wellness. Invite this information and conversations into your daily consciousness.

» Detoxify your body regularly. In ancient times, our ancestors didn't have to worry much about toxins. Their air and water were clean, their food was unprocessed, and there were no such things as industrial chemicals. My, how things have changed. You should detox your liver, kidney and colon twice a year and practise taking on board a glass of green smoothie every day that includes chlorella, spirulina and/or plant chlorophyllins.

» Improve your fibre intake. This keeps waste materials moving through your body effectively, and helps control cholesterol. You should be going to the lavatory once a day to clear your bowels. The accepted range is between three times a day to three times a week. This is individual, however three times a week is the bare minimum to prevent ill-health – a far position from enjoying optimal health. Regular evacuation of the bowels prevents blocking, backup, bloating and abdominal distension! Try psyllium husk powder, metamucil or a few organic figs or prunes with breakfast for a spring clean.

» Don't eat mindlessly at your desk, on your phone or watching TV. Know that everything we put in our mouths affects our brains first.

» Drink pure water; invest in a distiller or quality water filter. Most ground water is contaminated with man-made chemicals, as well as those that are added to it to clean it up. Combined with the overload from processed foods, this makes it impossible for the body to detoxify itself effectively.

» Are your body fat percentage levels down at the correct level for your optimal health? Body composition is a far more relevant marker of good health and shape than BMI rankings. Check where you rate against the guidelines in this book. Mortality increases with fat weight.

» Exercise hard so you work up a sweat for 45 minutes at least five times a week. Always seek variety in your workouts, and push yourself to improve your performance.

Wealthy Body Wisdom: A great body operating at peak performance is a powerful business tool, a status asset and a longevity machine. Something to be proud of, that no amount of money can buy!

Level 3: Optimise Your Lifestyle

» Limit your use of antibiotics, steroids and anti-inflammatory drugs. Seek to build strength and internal host resistance to protect yourself from injuries, illness and disease.

» Eliminate your toxic body burdens. Toxins are molecules that mutate genes or disrupt normal healthy cellular function. These can be inhaled (as in the case of air fresheners, antiperspirants and other household aerosols), absorbed through the skin or taken into the body through food and drink. Lower your toxin and xenoestrogen levels by not cooking or microwaving with plastics; phthalates and xenoestrogens, both found in soft plastics, mimic and disrupt hormonal levels. Avoid ingesting pesticides. Remember, the residues of pesticides on fruits and vegetables can't always be washed off. Avoid heavy metals, including mercury from eating fish, elements from exhaust fumes, and cadmium from road tyre abrasions. Avoid some domestic cleaning products, and aluminium and non-stick cookware. We absorb these disrupters into our systems every day and they accumulate, causing problems throughout the body, from disrupting brain functions to damaging fertility and immunity.

» Spring clean your parasites. We may not like the fact that we share our bodies with millions of other organisms and, while some of them are classed as bacteria, others such as worms and yeasts place a strain on our bodies. The symptoms of parasitic infestation can be experienced as lethargy, depression and fatigue. Parasites should be purged regularly from your system. As there are a wide variety of remedies available, ask your doctor or natural health practitioner which would be best for you.

» Boost your immunity. Good immunity is critical; it keeps us free from disease and ensures that we remain strong and healthy. To support a top-performing immune system, your body relies on a ready supply of nutrients to allow chemical reactions to take place billions of times every second.

» Upgrade to a range of high-quality, anti-ageing support supplements. A specialist anti-ageing physician will be able to advise which supplements you need to take based on tests and examination, and may prescribe them for you. When it comes to purchasing any supplement yourself, do your research on the brand to check it has an impeccable reputation for quality ingredients and formulas. Sometimes it's actually true that you do indeed get what you pay for...

» Get yourself completely overhauled. Everyone has their own individual issues, whether it is still carrying too much weight, lower back pain, allergies, aged skin or maybe even a concern about something in family history. This should spur you on to take measures to get these issues sorted as soon as possible to improve and prevent disease. We recommend requesting an endoscopy (visual examination of the oesophagus and stomach), colonoscopy (large intestine), and prostate check if you're a male over 40. There you go – a treat for your 40th birthday.

» Never mindlessly go on medication without thoroughly researching the effects, side effects and efficacy from credible independent sources.

» Check the ingredient list on all your food. If it has one, don't eat it.

» Get your moles checked and have your teeth examined. People with gum disease are more likely to suffer narrowing of the arteries because bacteria from the gums enter into the bloodstream and can cause inflammation in the arteries. Turning back your age clock is all about prevention and early detection, so have a full health check with a specialist anti-ageing doctor, dentist and endocrinologist.

Optimise Your Brain Function

In the quest for a really healthy body, one of the most overlooked areas is the brain. Studies suggest we start to lose our edge around the age of 40 when the brain shows signs of slowing down. Even at this early age many will experience some symptoms of mental deterioration, such as impaired concentration, short-term memory loss and difficulties learning new information. The delicate balance of neurotransmitter production in the brain can be altered by hormone imbalances, chemical pollutants, medications or the choices we make regarding what we eat and drink.

Whenever you drink too much alcohol or you skip a nutritious meal, you are not only depleting your body but also starving your brain. It can take just a short time to see some of the effects: irritability, forgetfulness or food cravings. A normal brain processes a single thought at roughly one third of a second and unfortunately the difference between a sharp mind and senility is only a matter of milliseconds. Your brain speed is based on how quickly these electrical signals are processed. This rate is your real brain age, which can be quite different from your chronological age.

You can help safeguard against dementia, depression and other brain disorders by taking better care of yourself earlier on in life. Creating a healthy brain begins with plenty of exercise, as it needs a constant supply of healthy, rich blood bringing oxygen and nutrients. Next, a diet of high-quality proteins, a wide variety of vegetables and quality omega-3 fats, as the brain runs on glucose and is built on fats, cholesterol and proteins. Thirdly, take a vitamin supplement in addition to your diet, and finally, fuel your on-going thirst for knowledge by reading widely and seeking out new information. What is good for the body is always good for the brain!

Consume more high-quality oils in your meals:

> » linseed oil
> » coconut oil
> » avocado
> » grass-fed butter
> » raw olives
> » nuts and seeds

These all have powerful nutritional benefits while keeping you feeling satisfied for longer. They give you energy without having to resort to sugar and processed grains. Remember, just because an oil says it's 'vegetable', does not mean it is healthy!

Supplements for the brain include DHA and EPA – Docosahexaenoic acid (DHA) and Eicosapentaenoic acid (EPA), Phosphatidylserine and Acetyl-L-Tyrosine.

> » DHA represents up to 97 per cent of the omega-3 fats in the brain
> » DHA and EPA enhance focus
> » DHA and EPA improve tolerance to stress

Phosphatidylserine:

> » improves short-term memory and recall
> » enhances focus
> » leads to better co-ordination
> » improves adrenal stress response

Acetyl-L-Tyrosine is found in dairy products, meats, fish, eggs, nuts, beans and oats. It:

» improves blood flow to the brain
» increases neurotransmitter production
» is used to treat depression, ADD, ADHD, PMS, Parkinson's, Alzheimer's and ED

Maintain Your Hormones

The endocrine system is a group of glands that manufacture and secrete powerful chemical messengers called hormones. The glands orchestrate together, 90 per cent under the direction of the brain, controlling everything in your body from your reproduction cycles, skin thickness, memory, muscle tone, cell renewal and organ condition, to when you go to sleep and when you wake up. Our hormone levels decrease with age, which clearly has a profound effect on how we look, feel and function.

Beginning between the ages of 30 and 40 your oestrogen, progesterone and testosterone levels start to fall. Don't throw your hands up in horror as you get mood swings, hot flushes or start losing interest or ability in sex. Learn as much as you can about this area of your health, and what can be done to minimise this damage. Have your hormones checked in your mid-twenties so you have a reference profile to check against later, and explore bio-identical hormone replacement if there is a need. (These are hormones made from natural sources, such as plants, and work as well, if not better, than the pharmaceutical variety, as they produce no side effects. Synthetic pharmaceutical hormones can also be patented, whereas natural bio-identical hormones cannot.)

Do bear in mind that checking your hormone levels requires blood testing and other monitoring by specialist health professionals, such as carried out by our medical director, Dr Sergey Dzugan (www.dzlogic. com). To have healthy hormones you have to have healthy glands, and to have healthy glands you need a healthy brain.

What is not widely known is that after mid-life (depending on your state of well-being and health), your main source of hormones, including progesterone, come from your adrenal glands rather than the testes and ovaries. Oestrogens are all about growth in the body, but it's progesterone that balances everything out. If, through prolonged or chronic stress, you have poor adrenal health and low reserves, your hormone output will also be compromised. By now you will know of many of the conditions and ailments this can bring about, including fatigue, headaches, allergies, unexplained weight gain, migraines, sleep disorders, anxiety, depression and mood swings.

One-and-a-half thousand biochemicals change in the body when you run late, take a bad phone call or overload on social media. Everything is intrinsically linked throughout your body – this is why diet and lifestyle play such an important part in healthy hormones. Intense weight training has also been found to have a rejuvenating effect on these chemical messengers, which is why we have made a point of including this type of exercise in our recommendations.

Be happy! Think young! We hasten our age clock if we spend too much time being unhappy, anxious, negative or pessimistic. Studies have also shown that a good mental attitude is imperative to ageing well. Staying optimistic and positive and knowing that life is a self-fulfilling prophecy is a key strategy. If we take responsibility for our own thoughts, mental alertness and happiness we can stay healthier and younger for longer!

Just by putting a few of these tips and techniques into practice, you'll begin to see results within a few short weeks...!

18.
THE WEALTHY BODY Q & A

This chapter answers some of the questions we have received from clients, readers and session attendees.

Eating in the Office

Q: **How do you deal with eating proper, regular meals when you're stuck behind your desk or in back-to-back meetings? It's difficult not to nibble on snacks when you're hungry, and often lunch is eaten at the desk as well.**

A: That's a common problem, especially when most snacks are 'low-performance' foods, and there's no real measure of how much you end up eating during the course of a day. To answer your question, it's probably easiest to just cut straight to our top 'best practice' strategies for eating in the office.

» Keep a bottle of water at your desk. (Don't buy commercial brands of flavoured or fruity water – they are full of sugar.) Sometimes perceived hunger is actually a signal you're getting dehydrated, so stay alert by taking on plenty of water during the working day. Whether in your office or working a trading desk, fill up a glass bottle with filtered water (a bottle is less likely to spill on your keyboard or phone, and glass is preferable to plastic), and pop in a wedge or two of lemon or lime, for a more interesting, flavoured and nutritious way of keeping your water levels topped up.

» Breakfasts are quite straightforward. Many food bars and takeaways now serve hot oatmeal porridge to go, and a paleo-style Bircher muesli is another option. Even better, if you're sitting down at a cafe, order an omelette, or scrambled/poached eggs with tomatoes, mushrooms and beans (high fibre, protein and some starchy carb energy).

Stay away from the 'beige' breakfast items such as Danish pastries, croissants, pain au raisin/chocolate, white toast or bagels – all are empty fast carbs that will only suck the energy out of you. Bad move at the start of a day. (Do we really need to point that out?)

» If there are no easily accessed outlets for healthy foods near your office, invest in high-quality food containers for bringing meals to the office from home. You can also buy containers for keeping soups, stews and casseroles hot all day, or your home-made super smoothie cool all day. Meals like that are easy to keep by your desk and take in small portions at any time without any additional preparation or heating. Successful physique competitors and athletes know they'll *never* reach their nutrition targets by relying on bought-in or eat-out food. Hard-boiled eggs are also brilliant to bring into the office, as you can eat them cold at any time, although your colleagues might disagree.

» If you're grabbing lunch at an eatery near work, buy two meals while you're at it: one to have for lunch, and one to eat later in the afternoon when your energy levels start to fall. The choice is wide, and can include dishes like chicken or shrimp salad, sushi/sashimi, three-bean soup, vegetable sticks with hummus, low-fat burritos, healthy wraps, hi-vitality smoothies and quinoa-based salads, just to name a few! (Watch out for some of the hot Asian dishes and some ready-to-go soups, though, as they can be *really* high in salt.) All of these are good to eat at your desk as they're portable and low mess! Stay away from sandwiches, which tend to include too much simple and processed carbs from the bread.

» If the office has a restaurant or canteen, avoid bread-based meals. Hot meals are usually fine, though: roast chicken/beef with steamed veg, soups (not creamy), stir-fries, custom wraps/burritos, etc. Most ingredients from the salad bar are great too, but stay away from too much cheese, instead opting for grated Parmesan (which has high flavour for lower volume and calories).

» Nuts and dried fruits are generally healthy, but be careful about eating too many. Remember: a small handful of raisins is a large bunch of grapes, a prune is a whole plum and a dried apricot is, well, an apricot. So, to keep your sugar intake down, eat only one or two pieces. It's also worth bearing in mind that a large medjool date has the same number of calories as a banana, and two glasses of fruit juice the same calories as a cheeseburger. Nuts are good energy and brain food, but again don't over-consume. Brazils, almonds and walnuts are best. If you're buying trail mix as an emergency meal (also great for when travelling), make sure it's only one of those single-portion-sized packets that may also include seeds such as pumpkin, sunflower or linseeds, and even 90 per cent cocoa organic chocolate.

» Things to keep in your desk drawer: a small bottle of balsamic vinegar or low-fat dressing; knife, fork and spoon; wet-wipes and tissues; a dessert bowl/small plate; green tea bags; organic oatcake biscuits; some fruit; small container of home-made trail mix; a can of tuna in spring water.

Q: How do you deal with extended meetings, when they only serve cookies, cakes and sandwiches?
A: If it's going to run through lunch or afternoon mealtime, when everyone else makes a dive for the sandwiches, break out your own meal. Everyone's going to be eating something, right? So you might as well eat healthy. If you have the seniority to do so, instruct corporate catering to serve something else. Ask for things like vegetable sticks with hummus dip, sushi, chicken salad wraps, fresh fruit, etc. Opting for nutrient-dense foods as opposed to nutrient-dead foods can be slightly more expensive, but it's also the difference between having your team highly energised, engaged and creative, or foggy-headed, fractious and unfocused. Which do you think will waste time, and cost you more money?

Eating with Clients

Q: OK, so what about a client dinner or meal out with your team?
A: Two issues here: food and booze.

» One of the keys to eating right when you go out to restaurants is remembering this: the right foods (variety); the right composition (protein, vegetables, carbs, fats); the right amounts; the right assertiveness; and the right times. When you keep those five elements in mind, you can almost always find something that will work for you. And if you don't – be assertive anyway and explain to the waiter or waitress exactly what you need.

» Task your assistant to find out (if possible) where your client dinner is going to be held, and to go online to check the menu options, or call the exec chef to find out what options they have that would suit. Have them text or email those options across to you so you know exactly what to order when you get there. They may have to pre-order a special dish for you, but then at least the restaurant is briefed and prepared and there's no fuss on the day. If need be, instruct your scheduling team to say you have an allergic reaction to certain sugars, fats, alcohol, wheat, dairy, nuts, or whatever it is you need to avoid or reduce. (This has proven to be such an important strategy that we now run special workshops specifically for PAs and EAs to instruct them on these skillsets.) It may also pay to let your client know that you only eat a 'high-performance' diet.

» When it comes to alcohol, there's a great deal of pressure in corporate culture to drink and get drunk as an act of collaboration and bonding. However, this will only compromise your performance the next day, and your travel schedule will be challenging enough without making it worse. If you're the most senior person present, toughen up and set an example.

» If your clients are entertaining you, go ahead and have a couple, but then pull the 'high-performance' card and switch to non-alcoholic drinks. Alternatively, play a more strategic game – drink sparkling water in a champagne glass; take a sip out of a full glass and then drink only water afterwards; or alternate one sip of wine with two sips of water.

» The bottom line is that other people cope where they have to (vegetarians, kosher, recovering alcoholics), so you can be inventive and play a smarter and higher game if you need to as well. An athlete doesn't drink alcohol before or during an event. Neither should you.

Business Travel

Q: How do you handle getting the right food when your first meeting of the day is a breakfast meeting at the office and they only serve croissants, pastries, toast and coffee?

A: The best way is to get up a little earlier and get room service to bring you a breakfast of porridge oats, Bircher muesli, an omelette, scrambled eggs or poached eggs with wholegrain toast. Stay well away from fruit juice, but instead eat a piece of fresh fruit on the way into the office. Even if you got in late the night before, getting up half an hour earlier to eat an energising breakfast is a smart strategy. If you have the luxury of a little breakfast time at the hotel buffet, ask for an omelette with lots of vegetables (onion, peppers, tomato, mushrooms). Alternatively, order scrambled or poached eggs to have with grilled tomatoes, mushrooms, beans and maybe lean ham. Often there'll also be hot porridge oats, sugar-free Bircher muesli or a dry Swiss muesli you could have with fresh fruit or Greek yogurt to get the day rolling, and you can always take a couple of hard-boiled eggs, a banana or apple with you when you leave.

Q: How do you cope with tiredness when your schedule is wall-to-wall from the moment you fly in to the moment you fly out and on to the next jam-packed day of meetings in another time zone?

A: Most times when we hear of this, it becomes clear that there is a failure to organise the schedule effectively, and/or a failure to train for the trip. Again, your EA needs to be fully briefed about your requirements when travelling, and they need to enforce your preferences with an iron fist! Your chain is only as strong as the weakest link, and you need to be performing right at the top of your game to be effective. Otherwise, the trip is for nothing!

> » You will need access to the right nutrition at the right times. You need your meals and events planned to allow you adequate refreshment breaks. Make sure you take all your supplements with you, including melatonin, 5-HTP and magnesium (to help you sleep), plus your multi-vitamin/ minerals and vitamin C.
> » You need one or maybe two 30-minute spaces somewhere in the day or evening for exercise.
> » And you need sleep. Catching up on sleep in the plane is not something you can guarantee, so it shouldn't be taken for granted.

» Before embarking on any business trip, you also need to make sure you've done your homework. In other words, you need to make sure that you are in peak physical shape. It's like an athlete going to the Olympic Games. You will need to be lean, strong, fit and healthy to endure the challenges that business travel throws at you. If you're not in top shape before you travel, you will struggle. You will under-perform. And you will come back in worse shape than when you left.

Our Top Tips For Travel

» As soon as you can, when arriving in a new time zone, get a workout in. This one strategy is the single most effective thing for busting jet lag. Even if there's no gym in your hotel (seriously?), you can do exercises in your room using bodyweight or bungy ropes, or even climbing stairs on the fire escape for 20 minutes. Do the same first thing in the morning and you'll be all set to go.

» Take 5–6mg of melatonin, 5-HTP and magnesium 30 minutes before going to bed.

» Take a hot bath before going to bed. This relaxes tense muscles, calms the mind and artificially raises body temperature. One of the key triggers to getting to sleep quickly is a drop in core body temperature, so raising it slightly higher creates a bigger, more dramatic drop, and thus a faster pathway to sleep.

» Don't drink coffee within six hours of going to bed, and certainly avoid any nightcap.

» Drink lots of water during your flights, and stay away from carbs, sugary drinks and snacks on the plane. During the day, drink green tea to help stay alert, eat quality protein, lots of fibrous (crunchy) vegetables and double-dose your multi-vitamins. If you are under stress/fatigue your body places a massive extra load on your immune system. Most multi-vitamins are created to cover RDA (Recommended Daily Allowance), which is formulated as a base line to prevent malnourishment only. Double-dosing is the least you could do to support this, and if there are surpluses of any particular vitamin/mineral, the body will simply excrete them.

The thing is though, because your meals will be different in composition from day to day, you have at least covered any possible deficiency, and as such this is a sound insurance policy. The body will have to work slightly harder to excrete these, but nothing near as arduous as coping with a glass of wine...

» Take time for a 'Deep Five™' (five deep breaths), neck stretches and regular toilet breaks – and stay as active and mobile as you can during the day.

» If you get constipated when travelling, take a mild herbal laxative with plenty of water to keep things moving. Stagnant material in your bowel leeches toxins into your bloodstream and will make you foggy-headed and sluggish.

» Delegate all your follow-up work to your EA so you have time to work on your exercise, energy and recovery rituals.

» Grab sleep wherever you can and whenever you can. Even short naps can make a big difference.

» Don't cram your flight schedule. You'll perform much better and be more effective at business when you're less rushed and stressed. Thinking you can grab something to eat in the taxi on the way to the airport is foolish, and you can guarantee there will be nothing useful to eat when you get there either.

» And finally, when you're travelling on business, remember that you are not away on holiday. You cannot afford the luxury of letting your guard down at any time. With all the additional pressures and challenges that international travel demands, you have to be right on top of your game at all times – even more so than when you're at home. It is our observation that being successful at mastering business travel and staying in great shape for business is the domain of only a few very disciplined, dedicated and switched-on individuals. Are you ready for that?

Cooking

Q: Do I really have to cook?
A: Cooking up a lean body is essential. We have clients who enjoy a fantastic lifestyle with multiple homes in various locations around the world. Their homes are designer-built and decorated, including the stunning kitchens

that would be the envy of any professional chef. The most unusual thing we've noticed here is that in many cases the appliances in the kitchen have never been used. Not the oven, nor the grill or even the hob! It seems that eating out is becoming the default mode of dining for more and more people every year.

Recent research published in the *European Journal of Clinical Nutrition* found that eating out at a restaurant may be just as bad for you as a fast-food meal. Perhaps the temptations of hot rolls, dessert menu and that extra glass of wine all combine to create the perfect dining storm. Either way, this is not the first study to suggest that eating at fast-food outlets and full service restaurants is worse for your health than eating at home. In February 2013 the USDA released a report that showed that over the last 40 years more Americans are defaulting to eating out, consuming 32 per cent of their daily calories away from home, up from 18 per cent in 1977–78. It found that those who relied on eating out ultimately consumed more saturated fat and sodium, and less dietary fibre than those who ate at home.[27] Similar trends were observed in the UK in the 2014 Expenditure and Food Survey.[28] To be on top of your game, avoid the temptations and hidden calories that will side-swipe you, and reacquaint yourself with the joy and creativity of your kitchen.

Dietary Supplements

Q: How do I pick a good dietary supplement?
A: Here's what we recommend:

1. Purchase your supplements as close as possible to their natural form. Choose concentrated whole food supplements rather than isolated or synthetic products. Vitamins and minerals in your body shouldn't be viewed as independent substances, but rather as a cooperative network of nutrients working together to be of most benefit to you.

2. Check that the utmost care has been taken in all phases of their production, from growing their ingredients, to manufacturing, testing for potency and quality control. Unfortunately there are some charlatans out there who are only involved in the industry to profit. Also be aware that some importers and retailers of natural products trust the lab results provided by the manufacturers and exporters without checking or validating them.

3. Select from a range of companies that have a long track record of providing high-quality products that produce good clinical results. Know where they have been made, rather than packed. Many different brands can be still be tracked back to just one country or one source. Look for evidence of independent testing. We belong to a subscription site www.consumerlab.com. There are other sites also that give good independent reviews of popular supplement lines.

The Impact on Your Business

Q: Why is any of this relevant to my business? We don't have any major health issues on my team.
A: Really? Did you know that for every 10 Senior Managers in your business:

9 are already feeling the effects of burnout to some degree...

8 are failing to prioritise healthy behaviours in their professional and personal lives

7 are disengaged, or actively disengaged, meaning that only three are functioning effectively in their roles

6 are taking time off work for stress-related reasons

5 say that stress is damaging relationships with colleagues and clients

4 lose sleep worrying about work, and will want to leave your firm in the next two years

3 are overweight or obese

2 haven't had a medical examination in the last five years, and

1 will die from a stroke, heart attack or cancer due to work-related stress...

Not only that, but on average: two key earners will leave your firm this year, one because the competition has more attractive benefits. You will also spend half a million dollars, and nine months of wasted downtime finding and recruiting suitable replacements.*

It doesn't have to be that way...

*Statistics taken from *Management Magazine, Director Magazine,* The Hay Group Research, Gallup Research, Humanresourcesonline.net, Singapore Human Resources Institute, *Harvard Business Review, Singapore Business Review*

Did you also know that for every 10 Senior Managers who follow The Wealthy Body protocols:

9 manage their stress more effectively, and have energy to spare at the end of the day

8 enjoy a more satisfying work-life balance

7 successfully lose weight, get fit and reduce their risk of illness and disease

6 sleep better and say they are more refreshed when they wake up in the morning

5 reduce their alcohol intake and caffeine dependence

4 improve their mental agility, clarity and resilience

3 increase their capacity for current workload demands

2 take on more senior and visible roles in the company, and

1 will improve their golf swing and be longer off the tee ...**

Which set of numbers would your shareholders like to read?

**Statistics taken from Institute of Physique Management client data, harvested from over 15 years of detailed physical assessment records, medical records, and comprehensive client interviews, surveys and research.

The Wealthy Body Kicker

We chose the title of this book after much thought, care and deliberation. Of course we wanted you to pick it up and read it. But more than that, we wanted you to reframe the concept of well-being in business, understand the principles put forward and follow the advice we recommend. In doing so, we're convinced you can live a longer, active, healthy and more productive life, thus gaining the ability, capacity and functionality to accomplish all you want to achieve in the years you have. By now we hope you 'get' that.

But it's just the first step.

Now we have your attention, there's something else we want to tell you. In working with hundreds of business leaders over the years, we've discovered that there's a point where high achievers in business realise it's not about the money anymore – it goes deeper than that.

You see if you're at the top of your game, The Wealthy Body will extend your influence for longer, and also wider and deeper into society. It will enable you to inspire, change and shape the business and social communities of tomorrow. Instilling values, setting standards – and changing the future.

REFERENCES

1 Central obesity and increased risk of dementia more than three decades later, R.A. Whitmer, PhD, D.R. Gustafson, PhD, E. Barrett-Connor, MD, et al. *March 26, 2008, Neurology®*, the medical journal of the American Academy of Neurology,

2 Alcohol-Attributable Cancer Deaths and Years of Potential Life Lost in the United States, David E. Nelson, et al. *American Journal of Public Health*. April 2013, Vol. 103, No. 4, pp. 641–648. doi: 10.2105/AJPH.2012.301199

3 Ibid

4 Effects of eggs on plasma lipoproteins in healthy populations, M.L. Fernandez *Food and Function*, November 2010, 1(2):156-60

5 Glycaemic index and glycaemic load of breakfast predict cognitive function and mood in school children: a randomised controlled trial, R. Micha, P.J. Rogers and M. Nelson. *British Journal of Nutrition*. November 2011, 106, 1552–1561 10.1017/S0007114511002303

6 Exercise enhances the proliferation of neural stem cells and neurite growth and survival of neuronal progenitor cells in dentate gyrus of middle-aged mice, W. Chih-Wei, C. Ya-Ting, Y. Lung, et al. *Journal of Applied Physiology*, 2008;105:1585–1594

7 Exercise-induced promotion of hippocampal cell proliferation requires â-endorphin, M. Koehl, et al. *The FASEB Journal*, July 2008 Vol. 22, no. 7, 2253–2262

8 A Randomized Controlled Trial of High Versus Low Intensity Weight Training Versus General Practitioner Care for Clinical Depression in Older Adults, Maria A. Fiatarone Singh, et al. *Journal of Gerontology*: MEDICAL SCIENCES 2005, The Gerontological Society of America 2005, Vol. 60A, No. 6, 768–776

9 Acute hypoglycemia in humans causes attentional dysfunction while nonverbal intelligence is preserved, V. McAulay, I. Deary, S. Ferguson, and B. Frier. (2001). *Diabetes Care*, 2001, 24(10), 1745–1750

10 A high-fat, refined sugar diet reduces hippocampal brain-derived neurotrophic factor, neuronal plasticity, and learning, R. Molteni, R.J. Barnard, Z. Ying, C.K. Roberts, F. Gómez-Pinilla. *Neuroscience*, 2002;112(4):803–14

11 Vascular risk factors and cognitive function in a sample of independently living men A. Aleman, et al. *Neurobiology of Ageing*, April 2005, Vol. 26, Issue 4, 485–490

12 Diets Enriched in Foods with High Antioxidant Activity Reverse Age-Induced Decreases in Cerebellar â-Adrenergic Function and Increases in Proinflammatory Cytokines, Gemma Carmelina, et al. *The Journal of Neuroscience*, 15 July 2002, 22(14): 6114–6120

13 Cognitive Dysfunction with Aging and the Role of Inflammation, Arthur A. Simen, MD, PhD, et al. *Theraputic Advances in Chronic Disease*, May 2011; 2(3): 175–195. PMCID: PMC3513880

14   Health significance of calcium and magnesium: Examples from human studies, G.F. Combs and F.H. Nielsen. In: World Health Organization. Calcium and Magnesium in Drinking Water: Public health significance. Geneva: World Health Organization Press, 2009

15   3,751 magnesium binding sites have been detected on human proteins, *BMC Bioinformatics*, 2012;13 Suppl 14:S10. Epub 2012 Sep 7.

16   See note 6

17   See note 6

18   See note 6

19   Effects of High-Intensity Strength Training on Multiple Risk Factors for Osteoporotic Fractures: A Randomized Controlled Trial, Maria A. Fiatarone, MD, William J. Evans, PhD, et al. *Journal of the American Medical Association.* 1994, 03520240037038

20   More information on homocysteine can be found here: http:/www.homocysteine.org.uk

21   Homocysteine and cardiovascular disease: evidence on causality from a meta-analysis, Wald, et al. *British Medical Journal*, 2002 November, 23;325(7374):1202

22   Gangwisch, et al. *American Journal of Clinical Nutrition*, 2015 AJCN103846

23   http:/www.ncbi.nlm.nih.gov/pmc/articles/PMC3138025/

24   *Journal of Australian College of Nutritional & Environmental Medicine*, April 2002, Vol. 21 No. 1, 3–8

25   See note 2

26   The Health Benefits of Citrus Fruits, Dr Katrine Baghurst, PhD. CSIRO Health Sciences & Nutrition Project Number: CT02057

27   https://www.ers.usda.gov/amber-waves/2013/february/americans-food-choices-at-home-and-away

28   Official data on families' shopping habits between 1974 and 2014. The data, released by the Department for Environment, Food and Rural Affairs (DEFRA) and analyzed by the Open Data Institute, comes from food diaries filled out by families over 40 years. It came from the Expenditure and Food Survey, the successor to the National Food Survey, in which people were asked to submit diaries of what they bought from shops, or ate at restaurants for two weeks

ACKNOWLEDGEMENTS

Over the last three decades we have been privileged to work and move in the most amazing circles, and to study and learn from the best in the medical, health, fitness and corporate wellbeing industries.

We have spent, and continue to invest, much of this time with executives and business leaders who totally 'get it', and who see their bodies as part of their personal success arsenal.

It has been through these most valuable experiences and interactions that we have been able to imagine and create the concept of *The Wealthy Body in Business*, and we would like to thank all those who have played a part in its inception.

Healthy leaders create healthier businesses that produce healthier employees, families and, by social osmosis, healthier and more productive communities. To the companies that have opened their minds and unlocked the amazing energy and benefits of better health in business, we thank and applaud you for your forward-looking view.

Also our eternal gratitude to Steve Prentice, without whose efforts, guidance and prosaic magic we would never have been able to turn our unformed mountain of jumbled data, research, experiences and advice into something that resembled a proper manuscript. Well done that man.

And finally to our wonderful publishers, Bloomsbury, who took a punt, picked us up and brought this book to life – our heartfelt thanks to you all. Especially Nigel, Charlotte and Sarah for your faith, support, encouragement and advice along the way.

ABOUT THE AUTHORS

Longevity Specialist, keynote speaker and TV presenter Tim Bean, and author, researcher and health club owner, Anne Laing, bring together two vastly different worlds: the corporate health and wellbeing world, and the weight-loss, anti-ageing and beauty world.

Both are frequently called upon by the media for interviews and comment (*FT Weekend, Daily Telegraph, Evening Standard, Daily Mail, Sunday Times*, London *Metro*, ITN News, London's Capital FM, Sky1 TV, GMTV, Lorraine Kelly Today), and have been consulting authors, contributors and feature subjects for CBS News, UK *Health and Fitness* magazine, *Sunday Times Style* magazine, *The London* magazine, *Tatler, She, Ultrafit* and *Zest* magazines.

Tim also co-presented an 8-episode series for Channel 4 Television, 'Turn Back Your Body Clock' and the couple's subsequent book, *Turn Back Your Age Clock* (Hamlyn), a practical guide to de-ageing, was an international success.

For the last 25 years they have occupied a unique position – bridging the knowledge gap between medical, health and longevity and earning capacity, wealth and the business bottom line.

Their private clients include celebrities and social high-flyers, and their corporate clients include key earners in seven of the world's ten biggest investment banks.

Tim is on the senior faculty for Duke Corporate Education, is an Adjunct Professor at SMU, and speaks at corporate events, medical conferences and business universities around the world.

INDEX